CLIFF THORBURN'S
SNOOKER
SKILLS

Edited by
Peter Arnold

Specially commissioned
photographs by
Peter Dazeley

HAMLYN

Acknowledgements

Photographs
Front and back jacket: Peter Dazeley/International Sports Book Network
All photographs by Peter Dazeley/International Sports Book Network
except the following:
David Muscroft Photography/International Sports Book Network:
pages 7, 9, 56, 84, 113, 114, 118, 119, 123

Artwork Mei Lim

The author and publisher would like to thank BCE for supplying the
snooker table for the photographic sessions.

Published by
The Hamlyn Publishing Group Limited
Bridge House, 69 London Road
Twickenham, Middlesex TW1 3SB, England
and distributed for them by
Octopus Distribution Services Limited
Rushden, Northamptonshire NN10 9RZ, England

First published in 1987
Second impression 1987
Third impression 1989

ISBN 0 600 55211 X

Produced by Mandarin Offset
Printed and bound in Hong Kong

CONTENTS

INTRODUCTION

There isn't a snooker player in the world who doesn't play better at one time than another – and there isn't a snooker player in the world whose game is so good that it can't be improved by more study and practice.

Snooker looks a simple game. After all, it requires only the ability to hit a ball straight. And when a professional is compiling a big break, an illusion is created that almost anybody could do the same. So why don't they?

The answer is that every time the professional player is faced with a shot, he goes through a routine that he has perfected through years of practice and experience. The experience helps his judgement in analysing the position and selecting the shot to play. When he gets down to play it, he puts into motion machinery that has been developed to maximum efficiency. From the leather at the tip of his cue to the soles of his shoes and their position on the floor, everything has been given attention and is calculated to achieve the intended result.

In fact, as you'll see later, I carry this picture of a machine even further than this when I play a shot: I include the snooker balls themselves as part of the mental picture. And when I set the machinery in motion, everything works – including the object ball dropping into the pocket – as if the whole thing had been designed and precision engineered by Rolls-Royce. At least, that's the idea!

If you're reading this book, then I assume you want to improve your game. Well, the first thing to emphasize is that there are no short cuts to success; there's no such phenomenon as a 'natural' player. Even Jimmy White had to practise for years to do what he does 'naturally'. But practice in itself is not enough. If you practise a cueing action that's fundamentally bad, you'll no doubt improve your game, but you won't become as good a player as you might have been with a little guidance.

Practice must also be fun. If you understand what it is you are practising, and why, you'll retain your enjoyment and enthusiasm. If practice becomes an aimless knocking about of the balls, it will become boring; you will consciously or subconsciously begin to think of it as a necessary chore – and you'll be largely wasting your time. You won't improve much.

When I started round about 1964 in Victoria, British Columbia (I soon took off for Toronto), I was lucky to have two good pals, Ike Pauls and Steve Boziak, who practised with me. We were so mad about snooker that we had little time for anything else. If we were not practising or playing we'd probably be sitting up talking about the game till 2 or 3 in the morning. I can't tell you how much it helped me to be around people who were keen and who talked with enthusiasm.

What should you practise? Since snooker was invented about 100 years ago, the experience of millions of players has indicated that some ways of doing things work better than others. Certain basic techniques have arisen. A new player can save himself years by adopting the stance that champions like Joe Davis and others since have perfected for him. You might say, correctly, that my style of play and that of Tony Drago, for example, are quite different, but in fact the differences are of temperament, manner and speed around the table rather than of basic technique.

Even established professionals return to practising the basics, particularly when they hit a bad patch. If something goes wrong with the machinery, it must be put right before it affects other parts. Just like the Rolls-Royce. In my case it is the position of the feet I adjust from time to time. I think this is because I have a dominant left eye, and tend to get out of position as I favour it in sighting the ball.

In this book, therefore, I've started by dealing with the basic techniques, since they must be mastered before it's worth even thinking about the spin, snookering, tactics and the rest that follows. Develop a well-grooved technique and anything is possible. Without it you can go only so far.

It follows, too, that a casual read of this book will give you an appreciation of the game and its subtleties. But if you want to reach a standard where you could win a competition or two, total dedication to learning from it is necessary.

How far can you go? Well, to get to the very top you need five qualities: the physical co-ordination of hand and eye to enable you to execute the shots; the dedication which will keep you enthusiastic and grant you the will-power to practise well when other

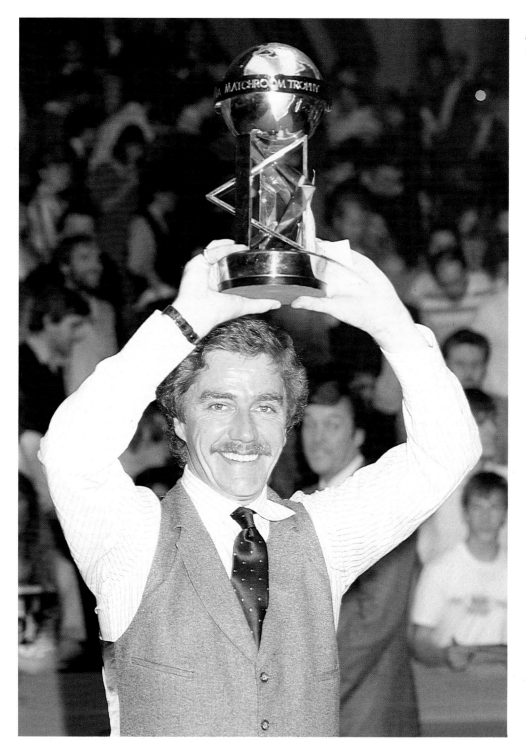

One of the results of all the dedication and practice – the Goya Matchroom Trophy in 1986.

attractions might beckon; the technique which comes from proper learning and practice; the tactical sense which comes from a love and study of the game and which allows the right choice of shot and strategy; the mental toughness to concentrate and conquer nerves.

You already know how you stand on the first two points – and in any case I couldn't help you on that score in this book. But I can certainly help on the other points. And even if you don't go right to the top, the higher you go and the better you get the more you'll enjoy it. I wish you the best of luck.

THE CUE

The cue is the most important and the most personal part of your snooker equipment. You should have your own; always use it for play and practice and look after it very carefully.

The choice of cue is very much a personal decision. You must pick one with which you feel comfortable. However, there are certain guide-lines I can give you to help limit the choice.

The length you choose will be influenced by your height. Many cues are a standard length of 4ft 10in (147cm). One school of thought says these suit everybody, a short player simply holding the cue further up the butt, but I think a cue is so personal you should choose your own length. Ideally, with the butt resting on the floor beside you, the tip should reach to within 2 or 3 inches (5-8cm) above the armpit.

The weights of cues vary, although most fall within a range of about 16 to $17\frac{1}{2}$oz (450 to 480g). A majority of the professionals use cues around this range, although Terry Griffiths uses a very light one of about 14oz (400g). Mine weighs 16oz (450g). Most of the good power shot players use cues of 18 or 19oz (500 to 540g).

As important as the weight is the balance. The best cues are made of ash or maple – ash has a much stronger grain – with the butts usually of ebony. The shaft is spliced into the butt, and the points of the butt represent where the point of balance should be. Be careful not to have too much weight in the butt, unless you see yourself as a power player.

The cue should ideally be straight, of course, but also slightly whippy in the shaft: you should feel a slight vibration if you smack your hand with it. Cues are not absolutely symmetrical when manufactured. Most good players look at the tip first, then look down the shaft with the butt at their eyes to test the straightness. Rolling the cue on the table doesn't tell you much, although you often see people doing it.

The cue should taper smoothly and evenly from butt to tip end, and at the tip end should have a metal or bakelite ferrule to protect the wood when tips are removed or attached. The diameter at the tip end is usually 10mm, which I advise. The old imperial tip of $\frac{3}{8}$inch is slightly less at 9.52mm. Another standard size is 11mm. I remember playing the professional Les Dodd when he was having a lean time, and suggested that he might try a larger tip, as he was using a very small one. He did and hit better form immediately.

Two-piece and extension cues

Although two-piece cues have become widely used by snooker players only since the 1970s, my idol George Chenier, the old

The parts of the cue. Where the tips of the butt reach furthest up the shaft is about where the point of balance should be.

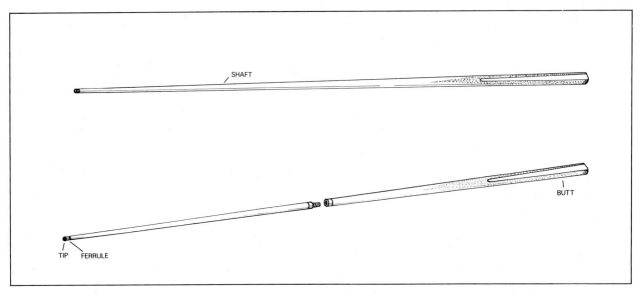

SHAFT

BUTT

TIP   FERRULE

Canadian pool and snooker wizard, used one back in the 1940s. He was the first world-class player to do so. In 1950 he made a world record break of 144 using one, and in 1958 he made 150 unfinished in the world straight pool championship. The tip end screws into the butt end at half way, both ends being again protected by a ferrule. The main object is easier transportation – obviously the cue will fit a case half the length of a 'one-piece' – but with some of these cues it's also possible to buy a special long butt-end, so that by unscrewing the normal butt-end and replacing it with the long one you can have your own extended cue. I've used my own two-piece cue for many years, and I suspect they will become more and more popular. I make my own extended cue by fitting the cue into my own butt-end extension, and I would recommend you to get one too. The cue is inserted into the extension tightened round it by a screwing action.

The tip

The tip should be domed and is again a question of personal choice. The amount of 'give' is what matters. Test a new tip by gently pressing a thumbnail into its side to get the feel of it. If a tip is hard, you might almost as well play without it, as there will be no grip on the cue ball; if it's too soft, it will feel like hitting the ball with a sponge, and it will be difficult to impart spin to the cue ball. You must decide the 'feel' you prefer and choose your tips accordingly.

It's useful if you can fit your own tips, because it gives you the confidence of knowing the job is properly done. The bottom surface of the tip and the end of the cue should be lightly filed to ensure they are clean and flat and the tip should be stuck on with a quick-drying glue or with the handy gelatine wafers which are specially made. These need slight softening in hot water.

The correct dome shape is achieved with sandpaper, preferably, or a file. Always shape away from the tip in the direction of the butt. An old shiny tip can be tapped with the file to roughen it slightly, but don't file it hard enough to upset the fibres.

In play keep the tip well chalked. Don't push the chalk directly on to the tip, but gently wipe the chalk across it – and frequently. Little and often is the rule.

The tip is crucial. It is, after all, your point of contact with the cue ball. If the cue is like your arm, the tip is like your fingers – and should be almost as sensitive.

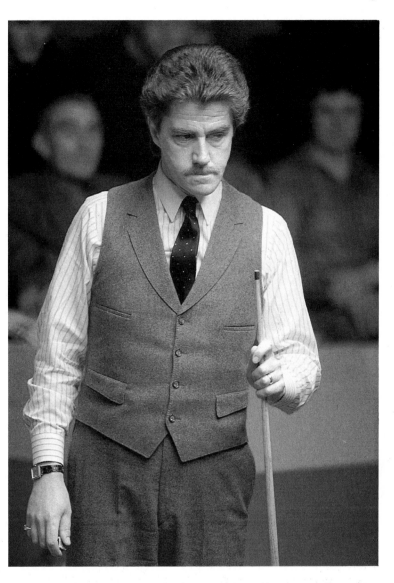

Care of the cue

Keep the cue clean and dry. An occasional wipe down with a cloth soaked in water will do no harm if it's well dried. It's not necessary to oil it (I don't myself) but a touch of linseed oil every couple of seasons would do no harm.

Treat it as if it were alive. Don't leave it by the fire to become brittle, for example. The easiest fault it can develop is a bend, so do not lean on it or even lean it against a wall. When it's not in use, keep it upright or lying down in its case. I remember Steve Duggan playing Ray Reardon in a qualifying match for the Rothmans Grand Prix, a world ranking tournament. The match was in a hall used for squash, and the walls were damp. Steve left his cue against the wall in an interval, and the tip got soaked. He had no chance from then on.

You can see from this photograph from a tournament that my cue comes to just above my armpit.

OTHER EQUIPMENT

Unless you're lucky enough to own your own table, you'll play on a variety of them, and soon discover that their characteristics vary greatly. Some will have a good 'nap' on the cloth, others will be worn; some will have firm cushions, others soft; some will be fast, others slow. You should play on as many as you can, but it's a bonus if you can play regularly on a good table, too. On a worn, shiny table it's difficult for even the best players to control the cue ball as well as they would like.

Pocket sizes vary, too. The standard width for tournaments is $3\frac{1}{2}$ inches (88.9mm), but the way the cushions are cut around the pocket, the undercut, makes some pockets easier than others. A player making his way is best served by playing with the largest pocket, to encourage his breakbuilding without putting too great a premium on potting ability alone. When a young player stops having to concentrate too much on the

pot, he can learn quicker what happens to the cue ball. He finds a new world opening up when he begins to be confident about making breaks, and the game becomes truly pleasurable. Like most top players I learned on tables with big pockets, and the table I practise on now, an ex-world championship qualifying one, has slightly enlarged pockets.

Tables should be regularly brushed and ironed. Ironing is always from baulk end upwards, in the direction of the nap. Never, ever, smoke at the table or stand drinks on the sides. Hot ash or spilt drinks are more likely to damage the cloth than the beginner's traditional and largely false fear of ripping it with his cue.

It's best to play on a full-size table, but I'm not against a smaller one, particularly for youngsters who are still growing. After all, managing the cue is the same on any size of table. I would suggest, though, that youngsters playing on a small table (8ft × 4ft or even 10ft × 5ft) use fewer reds. Six is enough – at the most ten. Otherwise the table gets cluttered up.

Tables for professional competition are assembled by specialists at the venue. The 'bed' is formed by five 2 inch (5cm) thick slates weighing 4cwt (200kg).

Snooker balls are made of a resin compound, which some time ago replaced the original ivory. The best tournament balls are Super Crystalate. They are made in matching sets with very strict weight tolerance (3g over the whole set), so sets should not be mixed. The reds are set up in position before the game with a triangle, a frame normally of wood.

Various rests are at the disposal of the players. The normal rest is used for shots otherwise unreachable, and there is a special long rest, called the half-butt, which is used for those shots which cannot be reached even with the normal rest. The half-butt is accompanied by its own cue, but many players (myself included) nowadays prefer to use it with extensions to their own cues. The spider rest is used for shots where a high bridge would be necessary, and the extended spider is used to carry the cue over a number of intervening balls. There's also a swan-neck rest for much the same purpose.

$12\frac{3}{4}$ in (320mm)

2ft 11in (875mm)

2ft 11in (875mm)

11ft $8\frac{1}{2}$in (3500mm)

$11\frac{1}{2}$in (292mm)

29in (700mm)

5ft 10in (1750mm)

The dimensions of a full-sized snooker table.

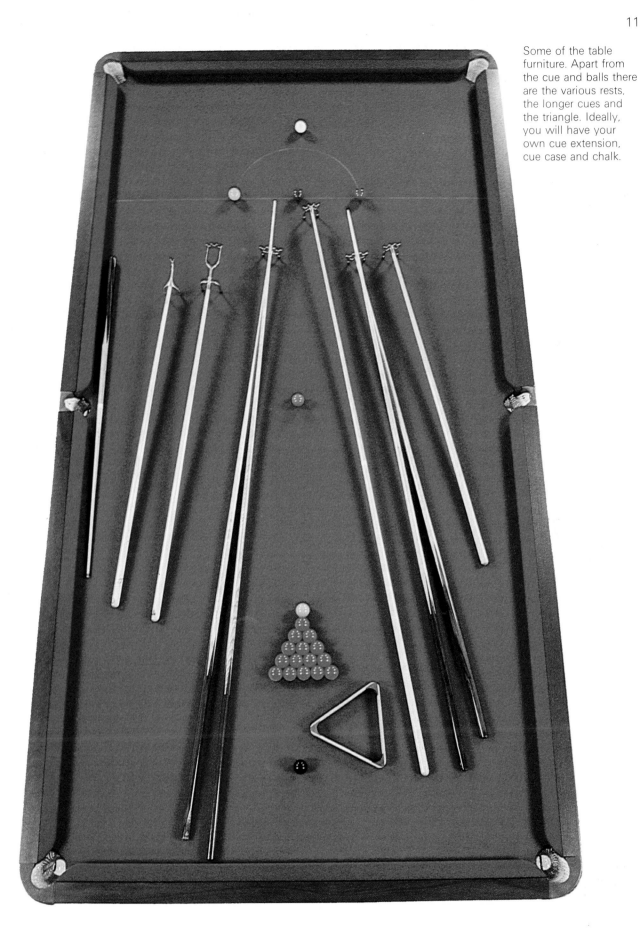

Some of the table furniture. Apart from the cue and balls there are the various rests, the longer cues and the triangle. Ideally, you will have your own cue extension, cue case and chalk.

GRIP

Lay your cue on the table. Now pick it up as if you are going to wave it across your body. The chances are that you have assumed an ideal grip for playing snooker.

The butt should be grasped 2 or 3 inches (5-8cm) from the end. The grip should not be tight, just firm enough to hold the cue horizontal. In fact 'hold' is a better word than 'grip', because the latter implies pressure, and your fingers should not be pressing into the cue at all.

The cue rests across the centre of all four fingers, and the thumb comes round, not so much to grip the cue tightly as to 'close the door'. The thumb rests against the first finger.

The fingers are together, and it's the first two, in conjunction with the thumb, which are really holding the cue; the third and fourth fingers are merely touching the cue at this stage.

When you're holding the cue at rest in your stance, the wrist should not be cocked, but vertical. In fact, looking at the grip from the back, it should be possible to draw a vertical line up through the end of the cue butt, the wrist and the elbow.

Another vertical line is that from elbow to wrist, looking from the side. In other words,

at rest the forearm should be vertical from all directions. Of course, once you start to play the shot, the forearm will move back, as on a hinge from the elbow, a movement discussed in the 'Striking the Ball' section. If you start with the forearm backward of vertical, you'll find that when you draw the arm further back to make the shot, you'll tend to lift the cue. If, on the other hand, you stand at rest with the forearm forward of vertical, you'll restrict your follow-through, which is important.

Common faults

One of the most familiar faults is to grip the cue either too lightly or too tightly. You don't want to hold the cue with the fingertips, as this will not allow you to generate any power in your shots, and shots like a deep screw must be played with power. Conversely, too tight a grip won't allow any 'feel' in the more delicate shots.

Another common fault is that of gripping the cue with the back of the hand facing upwards. This pushes the elbow into the small of the back and takes the butt too far from the body. Again there is a converse fault, where the hand wraps around the butt too far; this tends to push the elbow too far out and away from the body. This is perhaps not too serious a fault – anyway both Willie Thorne and myself are 'guilty' of it. Ideally, a good grip is one which ensures the cue goes through straight.

The feel of the shot

As you move the cue forward to strike the ball, your fingers should assume a *slightly* tighter grip on the cue, unless it is a power shot, when you grip harder at contact. It is this cueing hand which feels the contact between the tip and the cue ball, and as you play more and more you'll find that the idea of almost 'feeling' the shot as you play it is not too far-fetched.

Holding the cue further back

Some people prefer to hold the cue right at the end of the butt. I tend to move my hand further back for power shots. It's possible in this position to use the little finger at the back of the cue rather than wrapped round

I grip the cue a few inches from the end. The line from wrist to elbow is vertical.

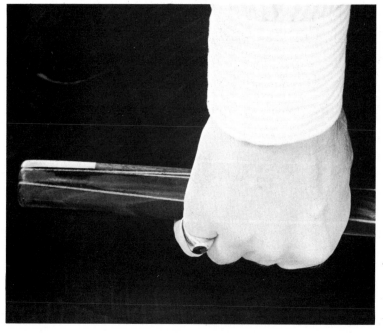

it. I don't do this myself but some people find it comfortable.

For very soft shots I move my grip further up the cue, so that I have a very short cueing action. The sort of shot which would require this technique is that where I have potted a red while playing essentially for safety (the shot to nothing discussed later), and have finished near the baulk cushion with a very difficult pot to follow if I wish to continue the break. The best option is frequently to roll up behind a baulk colour and leave the opponent a difficult snooker. The short cueing action helps to get the exact pace required on the cue ball, and of course this shot doesn't need a follow-through. In fact all cushion shots should be played with a shortened grip, for more control. It's the same principle as in my favourite sport, golf, where the putter and the wedge are the shortest clubs, because when using them you need the finesse and control.

THORBURN'S TIP

● *Few cues are absolutely perfect, so a good habit to get into is to hold the cue the same way up for each shot. Hold yours so that it is straight when you look along it. Note where the name-plate or some distinguishing grain is, and always hold the cue in the same way. Not only do you get used to the grain, but if there is a slight bend in the cue, it will not affect your sighting.*

Above left: The butt rests across the middle joints of all four fingers.

Above: The grip from above and behind.

STANCE

All that moves when you make a shot is your cueing arm, and if it pushes the cue through straight you will make a good shot. This is not easy unless you have a good stance: solid, balanced and comfortable.

Stance is very important. If you're a serious player you'll make thousands of shots during a year, and you should try to get into a groove so that all the preliminaries to the shot, like positioning the feet and getting down to play it, are automatic. Obviously, if you're going through the same basic motions thousands of times, you'll develop a skill and be able to perform much better than if every shot were approached in a different and haphazard manner.

The position of your feet is important because you must have a firm base for the only working part of the operation – your cue arm. I will assume you are right-handed, and left-handed players can easily transpose my remarks. Imagine that the line you're going to play the cue ball along (the line of the shot) is extended backwards behind the table. Your right foot should be on this line, with the toes pointing outwards, at about 45 degrees. This angle won't be the same for everybody – after all, some people are pigeon-toed – but it should be comfortable. The left foot should be *at least* 12 inches (30cm) away from heel to heel, and forward of the right foot. A line drawn from heel to heel should be at an angle of about 45 degrees to the line of shot. Again, this angle can be varied slightly: some players prefer a slightly squarer stance, others slightly more side on. The toes should point forward, parallel to the line of the shot.

In fact, I have changed the direction of my feet more than once in my career. At present I point *both* feet in the direction of the shot, but don't necessarily copy me – the right foot pointing outwards is more normal.

The hand on the table

When playing a shot you're like a tripod. Your third point of contact with the ground is your left hand, although this is of course through the table. The left hand forms the bridge, which is discussed in the next section.

There's a difference of opinion over the rigidity of the left arm in the stance. Traditionally the left arm has been thrust forward as far as it will go, with the hand the only contact with the table. If, as you read this, you push your left arm out straight and reach as far as you can, then pull your right hand back as if playing a shot, you will feel tension all along your left arm, which will tend to be forced out even further. This tension helps you to keep the body braced when playing a shot, and helps you to keep still.

However, I'm rather tall, and I find that bending the elbow slightly and laying the forearm on the table gives me both stability and comfort. You might try both methods. It does no harm to be comfortable in both styles, since sometimes it isn't possible to get the elbow on to the table.

In fact, as a young player, I read the book by Joe Davis which advised keeping the left arm straight. I felt the tension all right, but began to get back pains. I didn't realize for a long time that I was much taller than Joe. So I bend my arm where I can, and make sure my eyes are about the same distance from the cue ball as a short player's are.

The important thing about the bridging hand and the feet is balance. The right or back leg is rigid and more or less vertical. This is important. When you get older or tired, your stance will change. But you must make the effort to keep your back leg straight and rigid, otherwise things will go wrong with the shot. The left knee is bent and takes most of the weight of the body, which is to the left of the line of shot. The bridge takes its share of weight, too. When practising your stance, try lifting your bridge hand off the table; if you can do this easily, your weight is too far back on your feet. You should begin to fall forwards if your bridge hand is raised.

Common faults in the stance, relating to balance, lie in both legs being rigid, and therefore usually too far apart; both legs being bent; and the bridging arm not firmly based and wobbly.

The cue, obviously, is directly in line with the line of shot. It is also as horizontal as possible; in other words, it just clears the cushion. The position of the right arm has been dealt with to some extent in the section on grip. The right elbow and right shoulder are directly above the cue, and it helps to think of the right arm and the cue as one item, all in line and functioning as a unit.

The head is also on this line, directly above

the cue. And the head is right down so the cue almost touches the chin. If you have equal vision in each eye, then the plane of the cue will exactly bisect your face: in other words the cue will be directly under your nose and pointing in the same direction. Most players, however, and I am one, are stronger in one eye than the other, and will in effect 'sight' with one eye only. If you're among us you'll turn your head slightly so that your 'good' eye is directly above the cue. If you watch me play, or look at pictures of Joe Davis, you will notice we both sight with our left eye – Joe did so exclusively, while I tend to be not quite so extreme.

Checking the stance

The stance might be defined as the position you are in preparatory to striking the ball. The object is to be comfortable, balanced and in the right position to play the shot correctly. If the stance is correct, it can then be forgotten. You'll take it up instinctively and all your attention can be concentrated on your cue action.

While you're developing your style, however, it will pay you to check your stance from time to time. Look at the position of your feet; check your bridging arm and the position of your head; ask a friend to cast a critical eye at your overall stance. And, of course, if you ever suffer a loss of form, examine your basic stance to ensure that you are taking up the correct position. I check my stance occasionally, even after all these years, and still change it from time to time. It gives me something to think about and helps to keep me fresh and interested.

My stance. Note the vertical line from hand to elbow in my right arm, the back leg rigid and braced, the distance between the feet, the chin over the cue.

THORBURN'S TIP

● *Don't compromise on your stance: it's the basis from which all else flows. Don't say 'I'm short', or 'I'm tall', and therefore 'it does not apply to me'. The principles apply to all players, and time spent getting them right will save much more time and worry later on.*

BASIC BRIDGE

‘ Like Dennis Taylor and many other professionals I wear a simple ring on the third finger of my bridging hand. A few top players, like Alex Higgins and Tony Meo, wear jewellery on two fingers, so clearly it doesn't necessarily hamper style. I would advise, however, against chunky or flashy rings, to keep distractions to a minimum.

James Hunt, the former world champion racing driver, will not allow people to play on his table wearing a watch, in case they damage the cloth. ’

The most common photographs of snooker players in books and magazines, and the favourite angle of the television cameras, is the player about to make a shot. The easiest aspect of technique to study in pictures is therefore the bridge.

Many situations occur at the snooker table where a normal bridge is impossible, and adaptations of one sort or another are necessary. These bridges are discussed later. In this section I will simply deal with the basic bridge for an unhindered plain-ball shot. This is the one you will need most, and the other bridges stem from it, so it's necessary to perfect it.

A good bridge is formed by placing the left hand flat on the table with the fingers spread as wide as possible. If you then draw the fingers in very slightly, while keeping them straight, the knuckles will rise slightly.

The pads of the fingers, and indeed as much of the fingers as is possible from their tips, should be pressing very hard into the cloth, as should the base of the hand. The thumb is brought in as tight to the first finger as possible, and cocked. The base of the thumb should press into the cloth, but the thumb itself forms a 'v' through which the cue is guided. It's an advantage to have a very supple thumb (not to say a double-jointed one), but I'm afraid that's not

something you can obtain from reading a book.

Position of bridge
If you can satisfy all these requirements then you have a perfect bridge, but where is it formed in relation to the cue ball? As near as is consistent with a good backswing, or drawing back of the cue. You need to draw your cue back two or three times in preparation for a shot to make sure that the cue is moving on line. You've got to have as much drawback as you need to see this easily, so you do not want your bridge too near the ball, for then you'll have no room for this manoeuvre. On the other hand, too much cue forward of your bridging hand will mean you lose a little control, and the cue tip may wobble. Any slight inaccuracy at the bridge hand will be multiplied by the time it reaches the cue tip.

Some players prefer to be nearer the cue ball than others. The great Joe Davis advocated 12 to 15 inches (30-38cm), although at the same time he suggested withdrawing the cue only 5 inches (13cm). My own preference is to be closer than this, say 10 to 12 inches (25-30cm), with a slightly longer backswing.

A snooker teacher I knew, John Cassidy, nicknamed 'Doc', had a very long back-

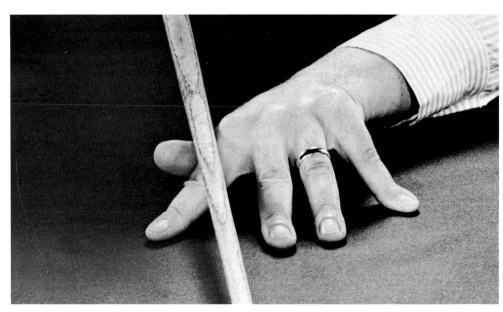

My bridge showing the cue passing over the 'v' of the thumb and the first finger.

swing which enabled him to put a terrific amount of side on the ball. Watching him once, and swaying as the ball took a wide angle off the cushion, I swayed so much on one shot that I nearly toppled over. Doc, unfortunately, did not reach the top because he could not produce his extravagant shots because of his long backswing especially when under pressure in a match.

Guiding the cue

With the bridging hand splayed, the cue will run across the first finger while the third finger should be pointing more or less parallel with the line of shot. The first finger and the thumb have contact with the cue and it's most important that they are firmly anchored, so check that the first finger and the base of the thumb are pushing down hard on the table.

Many inexperienced players do not pay sufficient attention to the bridge, thinking of it merely as something which separates the cue from the table. In fact it's very important in guiding the cue, and, since the skill in snooker lies in hitting the balls where you want them to go, the bridge is fundamental. A common fault is not to spread the fingers widely enough, so that an insufficient base is formed and the bridge is not quite firm. Another is not to grip the cushion firmly enough, particularly with the base of the thumb, with the same result.

Remember, too, that the bridge is your third contact with the ground, and that any insecurity here will lead to insecurity in the whole stance. When you approach the table, and have decided on the shot, your first action is to place your bridging hand on the table. The rest of your stance follows automatically – and when set you should be rock solid.

Notice how the cue is supported by thumb and forefinger but not guided. The base of the thumb is pressed into the table.

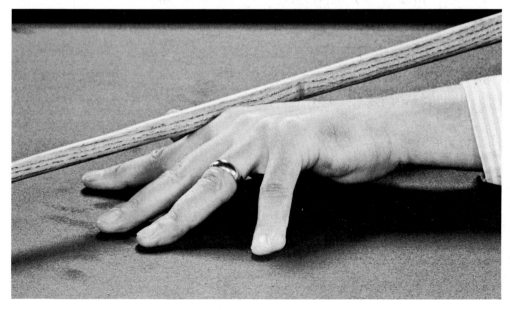

Notice how much of the fingers are pressed firmly into the cloth.

UNDERSTANDING ANGLES

There are still one or two aspects of the basic matter of striking the cue ball to consider, but let's digress a little to discuss aim. It's no good striking the cue ball perfectly if you can't work out in which direction to hit it.

Imagine an object ball, a cue ball and a pocket. Where must the cue ball strike the object ball in order to propel it into the pocket?

If all three are in line, there is no problem. The cue ball, aimed at the pocket, will hit the object ball directly in its path full on, and the object ball will assume the path of the cue ball into the pocket. This is called a *full-ball contact*, and it's very easy to see where to aim the cue ball.

But suppose the two balls aren't in line with the pocket. The cue ball has to hit the object ball off centre in order to propel it along a path at an angle to the path of the cue ball's approach. The illustration shows five such angles which snooker players talk about. We have mentioned full-ball contact, and from this it's easy to visualize *three-quarter, half- and quarter-ball contact*. The fifth such contact, which sets the object ball off at as near a right angle as possible from the path of the cue ball, is called a *fine cut*. Of course these terms are for ease of description rather than being mathematically correct. A shot will rarely be, for example, exactly a quarter-ball contact, but an experienced player will judge how much 'thicker' or 'thinner' he has to play to pot the ball.

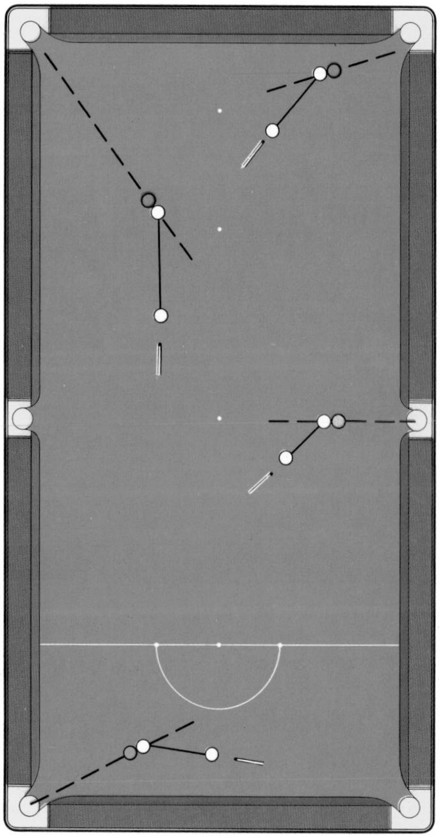

Finding the angle

Many players judge the angle by instinct, with varying success. They look at the cue ball, the object ball and the pocket, and estimate the angle. They then aim at a certain part of the object ball, which is again an estimate or guess. But judging angles doesn't come naturally, and it helps to get a feel for them by considering a more scientific method of judging the angle. It helps to consider what happens with a 'set' or 'plant' (see also page 62).

If two balls are touching, and are in line facing the pocket, and if the cue ball strikes the one further from the pocket, the one nearer the pocket will go into the pocket. This is not always exactly true, but for the purposes of this exercise, can be assumed as good enough.

Set up a red object ball and place the yellow touching it in such a way that it makes a 'plant' into the corner pocket. Strike the cue ball and, by hitting the yellow, pot the red. Then set the balls up again and look at the yellow from above the cue ball. The path that the cue ball must follow to hit the yellow full ball is, if not always exactly, then very close to the path the cue ball must take to pot the red object ball, even if the yellow were not there.

Look again from the cue ball to the red and yellow balls and you'll see the yellow overlapping the red in the manner of the diagram. The amount of overlapping will represent a half-ball, quarter-ball etc.

The area of contact

This, I think, is where the value of assessing the angle in this manner really lies. You

Four pots. The second 'imaginary' cue ball has been placed touching the object ball in a direct line with the pocket. It represents the contact the real cue ball will make with the object ball.

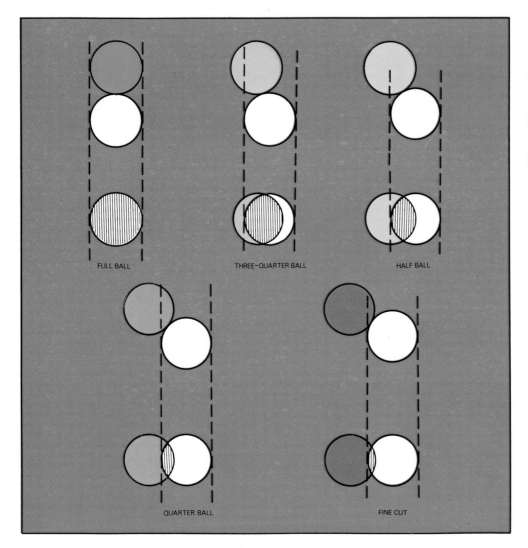

FULL BALL

THREE-QUARTER BALL

HALF BALL

QUARTER BALL

FINE CUT

The contact which the cue ball makes with the object ball can be described in various ways. The white is contacting the red at full-ball contact, the pink at three-quarter ball, the yellow at half-ball, the blue at quarter-ball and the brown at a fine cut.

perceive an *area* of contact at which to aim — a far more realistic target than aiming at a *point* on the object ball.

Describing this method of finding the angle sounds a little more complicated to describe than it is to practise. But in fact it takes no longer to play the shot using this method than it does to play the shot if you just estimate the angle and play it by instinct.

Judge the angle, in 'half-ball' terms, while standing looking at the shot. The over-lapping area is difficult to judge when you're down in the stance because the relative nearness of the cue ball makes it appear larger than the object ball. With experience these judgements will be made almost automatically.

It doesn't follow that the pot will be made automatically. Half-ball shots when potting almost parallel to a cushion are never easy, and quarter-ball shots are frequently hit just

too full, or slightly over-cut. But at least you have a picture in your mind of the target area, and you know how much of the object ball you are attempting to 'cover' with the cue ball. You can, in fact, visualize the path (its width is the width of the ball) along which the cue ball must travel to achieve this contact. If you have had difficulty in potting, this method of judging the angle is straightforward and could improve your confidence and success ratio greatly.

One rider might be necessary here, though. The nap of the cloth, and its holding quality, allow the balls to defy geometry to some extent, particularly with angles less than three-quarter ball. The speed of the shot will affect how much this phenomenon comes into play. If you find that on a particular table you tend to hit certain shots slightly too 'thick' (that is, not enough angle) then of course you must adjust accordingly.

SIGHTING

You've worked out the angle of the pot, settled comfortably into your stance, and your cue is resting in the 'v' of thumb and forefinger. Now, which ball do you look at when playing the shot – the cue ball or the object ball?

I'm often asked this question, and part of the answer is easy, part of it difficult. The easy part is where you should be looking when the cue actually makes contact with the cue ball: you should be looking at that area of the object ball you want to hit.

But of course you must look at the cue ball, too, when preparing to play the shot, and it's the 'switching' of the eyes between the cue ball and object ball which is difficult to define. If I stop to try to analyse what I do, I immediately suspect that the mere attempt leads to self-consciousness and that I'm not acting naturally because I'm watching myself! It's like trying to analyse how you keep your balance when walking – something which comes naturally immediately seems awkward.

When you're settled in your stance, the first ball you look at is the cue ball. You look at the spot where your tip will strike the white. Then you sight along your cue to the object ball, specifically to that area of the object ball you wish the cue ball to contact. If you look at the pocket at this stage it must be for the last time; the pocket is not now part of the picture.

A mental picture of the shot

Talking of pictures, at this stage you should have a mental picture of the shot you are going to play. This is a common technique in many sports, but is particularly appropriate in those where the striking of a stationary ball is concerned.

Since my early days in the game I've found it a great help to visualize the whole shot from beginning to end as if I were almost a spectator watching from outside. In fact, during my World Professional Championship match with Terry Griffiths, when I made a 147 break, I was reading a book called *Zen in the Art of Archery* by Eugen Herrigel (published by Arkana). I recommend it. The Japanese regard archery as an art and ritual rather than a sport, a ritual in which the highest Zen practitioner becomes independent of conscious purpose. Translated into snooker terms, the player and the shot become the same. The player, the cue, the cue ball, the object ball and pocket come together as if there were no distance between them, and the shot is made in the mind before you actually play it.

I'm not claiming to have reached this state myself, and snooker followers will remember there was nothing inevitable about the first red of that record break, which was – and I can hardly deny it – a total fluke. The point I want to make is that you must have an image of the shot you are making and you must

When sighting the shot I bring the tip of the cue up to about an inch (25mm) of the cue ball. Many players get closer, but my depth of vision is not too good, because of a dominant left eye.

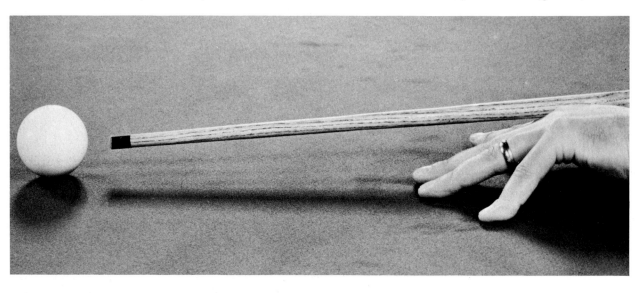

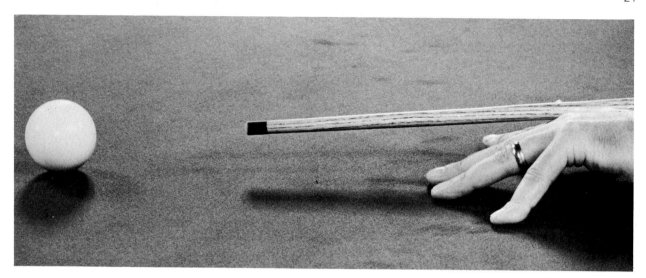

approach and play it with conviction. Playing in the general direction and hoping for the best won't help if you want to improve your game.

Before the shot

With this picture in mind, and with your eyes flicking from object ball to cue ball, and even further back to bridge and cue, move the cue backwards and forwards over the bridge in a smooth 'rehearsal' of the shot. This is known in the text books as feathering, and is an important part of the shot, or at least the build-up to it. During this manoeuvre you're checking that everything from bridge to object ball is lined up correctly and that the cue is coming through straight.

Important though it is, however, it's pointless to overdo this preliminary routine. A player who does is usually demonstrating nerves. After a time you'll probably find that your feathering technique becomes standard-ized (see also page 28). Some players bring the tip of the cue right up to the cue ball, so that it practically touches, but I've always been satisfied with a less extravagant feather. This is because my depth perception is poor, arising from my dominant left eye. I am frightened of touching the cue ball. I struggled on power shots because I could not follow through adequately. Also I had problems with the rest. Kirk Stevens pointed out how far I was from the cue ball before the 1983 World Championships, and I was able to make adjustments.

After the last feather, the cue arm is drawn back ready for the shot. I don't push forward immediately into the shot, in the continuous manner in which I have been feathering. There is a very slight, almost imperceptible pause. The eyes fix on the object ball. And the next move is striking the cue ball.

The distance by which I draw the cue back before striking the cue ball. As can be seen, it is not much more than 4 inches (10cm).

When playing a power shot, I draw the cue much further back – about 8 inches (20cm).

STRIKING THE BALL

' When I first started to play well (when I had made about five century breaks) I realized that the point of contact between object and cue ball is so small that it might just as well be a flat surface as a curve. So I started thinking of the two balls as cubes, not spheres, and I found that this made the whole process of striking the ball simpler, and I wished I had discovered this idea much earlier. '

We're up to page 22 already, and we're just going to hit the ball? Sure – this is a measure of the importance I place on the basic techniques. It's no good knowing what is meant by 'using check side to get on the black' if your stance or bridge is so bad you can't even strike the cue ball in a straight line.

We left the last section at the slight pause at the end of the feathering. To recap, you're settled firmly in your stance, the cue is as horizontal as you can get it and is running directly below your chin; everything is still, and has been since you began feathering, except for your eyes and your right forearm.

You now 'push' the cue through the ball. The action must be smooth, firm and positive. There must be no doubt, no tentativeness. You must strike the ball confidently, expecting it to go in the intended direction.

I wrote push *through* the cue ball, rather than *at* it, in order to emphasize the importance of the follow-through. But 'punch' is probably a better description than 'push'. The ball must be definitely struck, much like a boxer might punch his opponent on the jaw. In boxing, the forward momentum of the punch will continue after the jaw in its path has been knocked out of the way. The principle of the follow-through is recognized also in golf, cricket, tennis and other ball sports. The ball is struck in the middle of the stroke, with maximum efficiency, not at the end, when the stroke is winding down.

Players nevertheless vary in the amount of follow-through they employ. And the type of shot affects how much the cue goes through. The important thing is not how far you follow through but that you understand *why* you follow through. Don't think, 'I must remember to follow through', and push the cue forward as an afterthought. Regard the follow-through as part of the shot, and practise until it becomes a natural part of the cueing action.

Right-arm movement

At the other end of the cue is the only moving part of your body, the right arm. At rest before the stroke, as we have seen, the forearm is vertical. After feathering, at the end of the drawback, the forearm and wrist are at a different angle, and at the end of the stroke the arm has come forward and the elbow has dropped.

It's essential that nothing else moves. The head, feet, bridging arm and body remain absolutely still until after the follow-through. I advise not even looking at the path of the object ball into the pocket, if it helps. Don't be afraid of staying down on your stroke until after the object ball has been struck: it isn't posing. Watch the professionals do it (although it's not unknown for even the top players to slip up occasionally). It's a recognition that the whole stroke, right through to the end of the follow-through, is one smooth operation.

Lifting the head too soon to see the result of the shot (this is also true of golf and cricket) is a common beginner's fault and often leads to disaster.

Perfecting the cueing action

There's a simple practice for the basic cueing action, used even by professionals, though perhaps in their case it's more of a test to ensure that all is still well. The cue ball is put on the brown spot. The object is to strike it straight up the table over the blue, pink and black spots so that it hits the top cushion and comes back down the same path and over the brown spot again. It sounds easy but it's not – unless your cueing is correct.

Strike the ball in the dead centre, but don't concentrate too much on the ball for this exercise. Concentrate on your stance and your cueing action. Make sure the cue is straight and horizontal and moving smoothly through the ball. Keep your head down. Watch the tip of the cue. Don't strike the ball too hard – it's a difficult exercise for anybody to achieve with a power shot. Just play a firm, smooth shot, with enough power to bring the cue ball back again to baulk. If the ball does not come back over the brown spot, try to discover the fault.

If it goes off line going up the table, perhaps your stance is wrong or you are sighting the ball incorrectly. If the ball goes up the table over the spots but comes off the cushion at an angle, missing them on the

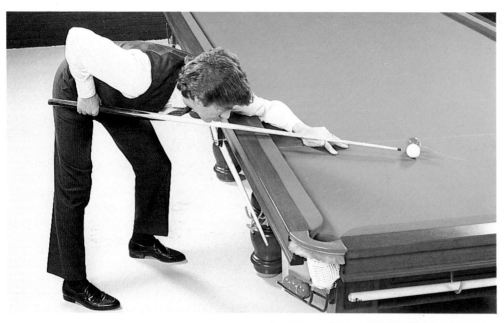

The whole stance before striking the ball. I am addressing the ball before drawing back the arm for the shot.

way back, the possibility is that you are not bringing the cue through in a straight line, and you're striking the ball off-centre, thereby inadvertently putting side on the ball.

I often see players who think they are striking the ball in the centre but are in fact striking it just off-centre, and I wonder if sometimes this might be an eye problem. If you find you have difficulty in potting the balls, try moving the point of contact of the cue fractionally to right or left and see if that solves the problem.

Practise this cueing exercise until you can achieve the desired result consistently. You'll then be ready to try some pots.

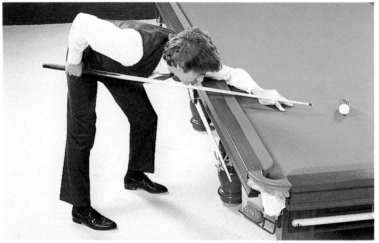

Above: After feathering, I have drawn back the arm. Here there is a slight pause before striking.

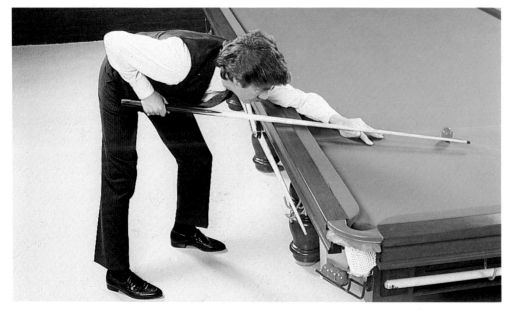

Left: I have made the shot. You can see from the position of the red ball how much I have followed through. I have just begun to raise my head. Notice that otherwise the right arm is the only part of the body which moves.

POTTING

In a frame of snooker, if a colour is taken with every red, there are 36 pots on the table. To win a frame at the top level you will need to score about 70 points, which, ignoring penalties, can't be achieved in fewer than 18 pots. So, no matter how good your safety, to be a winner you must be able to pot the balls.

When you're completely happy with your cue action, and can strike the cue ball so that it follows the path you want, it's time to introduce an object ball, and to practise transferring the impetus of the cue ball to the object ball.

We will concentrate on this first, without yet worrying about the third position which comes into the question of potting – the position of the pocket.

The object ball provides something else to look at when making the shot, and we have already considered in the section on sighting the problem of which ball we should look at.

A good first practice is to repeat the 'up-and-down-the-table' shot of the practice for striking the ball in the last section, but with a difference. The difference is the introduction of a red on the straight line up the table about 12 inches (30cm) from the cue ball. Make sure that the red is correctly positioned: if it is slightly off-line, the practice

cannot work. The object is to strike the cue ball dead centre, in exactly the same way as before. It will, of course, strike the red dead centre, propelling it up the table along the line the cue ball would have taken. The cue ball will follow slowly and, if both contacts are correct, the red ball will return from the top cushion on the same path and contact the cue ball at about the blue spot.

If it were necessary to play this shot in a match, when striking the cue ball you would be looking at the centre of the red. If you find this shot difficult at first in practice, you must try to discover what it is that you're not doing quite right, so you will have to attempt to see the action as a whole. Again, watch the tip of the cue, in case the cue is not coming through straight.

I wrote 'at first' in that last paragraph, because eventually you'll find that you can perform this shot. When you have a success rate of around 90 per cent, try the shot with

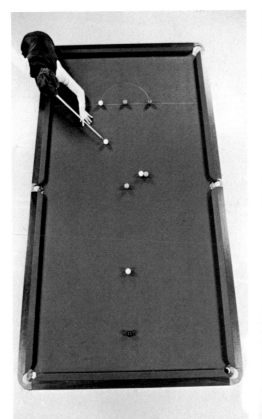

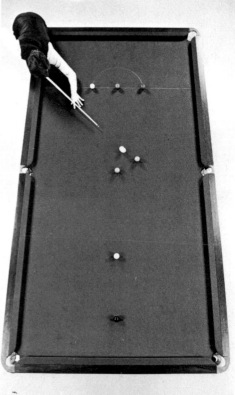

the red further away, on the blue spot. The principles are exactly the same of course, but the greater distance that the cue ball must travel before it hits the object ball affords more opportunity for error to creep in. However, properly executed, the red should return from the top cushion and meet the cue ball as before, but further up the table, nearer the pink spot.

Potting some long reds

When you have perfected that exercise, and can hit the ball in a straight line, it's time to try some straight pots. Place the red on the blue spot and the cue ball on the baulk line so that the pot into a corner pocket is exactly straight. Then move the red nearer to the cue ball, until it's about 12 inches (30cm) away.

The principle is similar to the last practice, but with two differences. First, you're not playing straight up the table, so your stance now has to be angled in relation to the table. Second, you have a third element, the pocket! In theory, this should present no more difficulty than hitting the centre of the top cushion, as in the previous exercise, but it is surprising what inhibitions an actual pocket inspires in a beginner.

If you can hit a cue ball into a pocket, and almost everybody can, you should be able to pot an intervening ball into it, too. Practise this shot as before, and then introduce more space between the red and the cue ball by leaving the red on the blue spot and the cue ball on the baulk line.

The greater distance between balls again makes it easier for error to creep in. If you're daunted by the distance between the balls and to the pocket, try picturing the shot as one item, as I outlined earlier. This helps you imagine a relationship between you and the balls and allows you to play the shot with more conviction.

Incidentally, the dead straight pot is one where I do allow the pocket to enter the sighting stage of the shot. Because the pocket and balls are all in line, a glance at the pocket in sighting gives a longer line on which to check that the cue itself is aligned. Bridge, cue ball, object ball, pocket, all receive a look as I prepare to play, but when the cue actually strikes the cue ball, I am looking at the object ball as usual.

Practise these pots into the corners from both sides of the table, and when you are proficient at them it is time to approach potting from another angle.

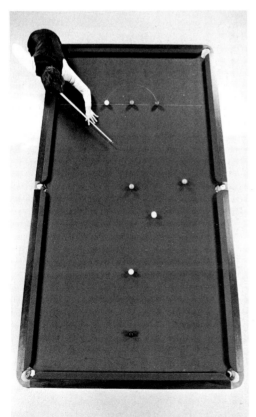 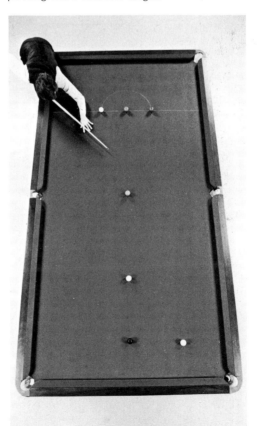

I am potting the last red at an angle (see page 26). *Left to right*: In the first photograph I have placed an extra cue ball on the table to show the contact needed on the red (see page 18). In the second photograph the extra cue ball has been removed, and I have struck the actual cue ball on a path to where it was. The third photograph shows the cue ball and object ball after impact, while in the fourth the object ball has been pocketed and the cue ball is approaching the top cushion. Notice that I have not yet got up from my stance.

POTTING AT AN ANGLE

' The difference between a straight pot and a fine cut into a pocket is less than 90 degrees. Between those two extremes, however, are an infinite number of angles. You must be confident at them all. '

We've already looked at the problem of finding the angle for a pot, and one hint of finding it was passed on, with a rider that it was to be used as an aid rather than an infallible method.

You're aware of the concepts of three-quarter ball, half-ball, contacts etc, and of the advantage of aiming at an *area* on the object ball rather than at a specific *point*. All you have to do to become proficient at straightforward potting at an angle is to practise finding the correct contact on the object ball. Once found, the ball has to go in, because your whole stance and cueing action is now perfect. If it doesn't then you must go back a few pages!

A half-ball shot is easy to define and to test its effects. On half-ball contacts, the centre of the cue ball is in line with the edge of the object ball (see the illustration on page 19). So to play a half-ball shot the cue, which is striking the cue ball at the centre, is

When you begin practising potting at an angle, place the object ball near the pockets as shown. You can set up these practice routines by using reds as cue balls if you like.

clearly pointing to the edge of the object ball.

To test the effects, place the blue ball on its spot, and the cue ball 12 inches (30cm) below it. Play a half-ball contact on the blue and note where it goes. Remember the angle. When you've played this shot a few times, and think you know the half-ball angle, put a red 18 inches (45cm) from a corner pocket, and then place the cue ball 12 inches (30cm) from it so that it's a half-ball pot. If you're right, you should now pot the ball with ease. Try the same shot on all six pockets.

Longer half-ball shots

When you've mastered the above exercise, play half-ball shots with the blue on its spot and the cue ball this time on the brown spot. The half-ball shot now is actually a slightly different angle because of the greater distance between the balls. Notice the path of the object ball as before, and then set up practice pots into the pockets as before.

It's much easier and quicker for me to describe these exercises than for you to practise them, let alone become familiar with all these pots, but if you are to improve your game you must master these straightforward pots. It is of course easier said than done, but we are back to my remarks about dedication in the introduction. You must practise to be good, and there are no short cuts.

You can probably guess at the exercises which follow. Having become expert at half-ball pots all round the table you can now make yourself just as proficient at three-quarter and quarter-ball shots.

Practising round the table

There are several practice routines which will help you to judge the angles correctly. One I like is based on the colours on their spots. It's always useful, particularly near the end of a game, to be confident about potting the colours from their spots. I would guess that about 90 per cent of amateur games are won and lost on the colours.

Start with the black, but as the black into a top pocket gives you a narrow target, begin with the black nearer the pocket than its spot. This opens up the pocket. Practise three-quarter, half- and quarter-ball pots into the pocket, then move the black away from the pocket towards its spot for further practice. As you get used to potting the black in each position keep moving it towards the centre of the table until it's on its spot. A good practice then is to arrange seven reds as cue balls around the black in an arc about 2 feet (60cm) from the black ball, so the two outside reds represent quarter-ball pots of the black into the pocket, the centre red represents a full-ball pot and the in-between reds represent half- and three-quarter ball pots. Practise potting the black with all seven red 'cue balls' in turn. In this exercise, and the remainder, always practise from both sides of the table, into each of the pockets.

When you are happy round the black, move down to the pink and arrange your arcs of red cue balls round the pink on its spot. You can practise at a different angle into the pocket, and from a longer range.

Having potted the pink into both top pockets satisfactorily, arrange your arcs on the top side of the pink on its spot, and practise potting the pink from various angles into the middle pockets.

Next, move down to the blue. With the blue about 12 inches (30cm) from the centre pocket, arrange an arc of red cue balls around it in the same manner, so that the centre red is a full-ball pot from the blue spot itself. In fact, it's a good idea to add two extra cue balls, one at each end of the arc, to represent fine cuts of the blue into the pocket. Having potted the blue from all nine

angles, move the blue ball onto the blue spot, arrange the arc again, and pot the blue from all nine positions. This time, with the blue further from the pocket, you'll need more accuracy.

Repeat the exercises with the baulk colours on their spots, potting them into each of the baulk pockets.

Of course there are all sorts of angles you can set up for yourself into any of the pockets. And I hope that you will, because it means that you've mastered the practices I've outlined and that you remain enthusiastic enough to seek others.

It's worth remembering that the angles are the same wherever you are on the table. It is a fact, however, that some players always tend to miss the same shot. Obviously there is a weakness in the judgement of the angle at one particular spot on the table. As the particular pot will appear only infrequently in matches, they might not notice for a long time that they regularly miss the same shot. Practice is where such things can come to light. If in practice you find difficulty with a certain angle, practise it until you discover the fault, and put it right. If you have a run of inconsistency, check on your basic technique.

THORBURN'S TIPS

● *Describing just one pot takes about the same time as a reasonable break would in practice. This rough check-list of how to do it is, of course, performed almost without thinking by an experienced player, because he has practised and perfected all the elements. No item is very difficult in itself; put them all together and you can pot snooker balls.*

● *A half-ball pot is a half-ball pot no matter where the balls are on the table, but the direction of the shot in relation to the cushion makes some appear different from others. Try to shut out everything but the cue ball, object ball and pocket in assessing the angle.*

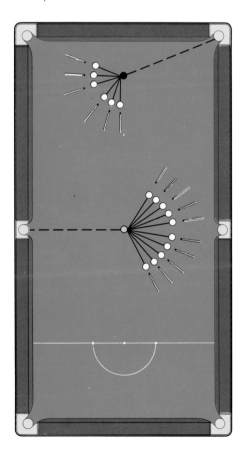

As you progress, the object ball should be moved further from the pocket, so that you practise potting the black and the blue, for example, from their spots at all angles.

PUTTING IT ALL TOGETHER

‘ When you see a good player in action, it appears he just gets down and pots the ball. Remember he too had to practise and polish each part of his technique before he could make it look so easy. ’

We've now reached a stage where we've practised all the basics, and can pot a ball without using spin and without any hindrances in our way. Before proceeding further, let's bring together the whole action of potting a ball.

Imagine you're going to pot the pink from its spot with the cue ball between the blue and brown spots. You approach the table, and you chalk your cue. You weigh up the angle of the pot. Is it a quarter-ball? Is it slightly 'fuller' or slightly 'finer'? Or, if you prefer, slightly 'thicker' or slightly 'thinner'. You make your judgement.

You decide where to place your bridging hand, perhaps some 10 or 12 inches (25-30cm) from the cue ball. You get your feet into the position of your stance. Your back leg is rigid, and on the line of the shot, with the toes pointing outwards. Your front foot is ahead of the back one, at least 12 inches (30cm) away, with the toes pointing parallel with the line of shot. The front knee is bent, the weight forward.

Your bridging hand has meanwhile formed the bridge, fingers splayed and pressing into the cloth, the forefinger and thumb forming a 'v' in which the cue is resting. Your bridging arm is either thrust out straight or is slightly bent at the elbow, with the forearm resting on the table.

You're gripping the cue firmly but not too tightly about 2 or 3 inches (5-8cm) from the end of the butt.

You bring your head down, with your chin at cue level. Your eyes flicker from the centre of the cue ball, where the tip is going to strike it, to the area of the pink object ball on which you have decided the cue ball must make contact (was it a quarter-ball, half-ball, something in between?)

You begin to feather, i.e. you push the cue forward almost to the cue ball and draw it back, perhaps 5 to 8 inches (13-20cm), two or three times, checking that the cue is straight on the line of the shot (see also page 21).

When the tip of the cue is practically touching the cue ball, the right forearm hangs vertically when viewed from the side.

The forearm also hangs vertically when viewed from the back, and indeed there are a

number of things in line here. If the line of the shot is drawn backwards, and given an imaginary vertical plane, this plane bisects the cue along its length, is on line with your chin and nose (unless you sight with one eye, in which case it bisects that eye), cuts through your shoulder, your elbow and your wrist, and also cuts through some part of your back foot. All these things are in line. Viewed from the front, the same continuation of the line of shot can be seen taking in your shoulder, elbow (not in my case, as explained earlier) and cue.

When you draw the cue back in your feathering, all the action comes from the 'hinge', the elbow of the cueing arm. The forearm moves backward, and the elbow has to move very slightly, almost imperceptibly, downwards to allow this. Nothing else moves.

It's noticeable that your cue is horizontal, and remains horizontal when you draw it back in feathering.

When you've made your final feather, there's a very slight pause – so slight that probably only you and I notice it. In this pause you look for the last time at the spot on the cue ball you're going to hit with the cue. Having decided on the angle, and got down into your stance, you probably haven't looked at the pocket more than once.

Now you punch the cue forward, as you do so transferring your attention from the cue ball to the target area on the object ball. The last thing your eyes are fixed on is the object ball. The cue remains horizontal and grooved in the line you've chosen for it. It strikes the cue ball firmly and follows through, finally stopping perhaps 8 inches or so (20cm) past where the cue ball was – perhaps slightly less for a young player. The hinge at your elbow has now almost closed, as your cueing hand has come forward, and your elbow has dropped to allow this. Nothing else has moved. It's a crisp, firm, positive, controlled, confident stroke.

Your head remains down, your body still, your eyes fixed on where the object ball was. Only when you hear the pink thudding into the pocket do you begin to rise from the table.

From this photograph you can see that I sight the shot mainly with my left eye, but the chin is well over the cue. The elbow should form a straight line with the cue, but over-enthusiastic pitching at baseball as a youngster has led to my slight deviation from the accepted ideal.

HIGH BRIDGES

You will frequently be forced into playing a shot with a high bridge. You will succeed if you play the shot with confidence and fail if you play it with anxiety. The confidence comes from practising the right techniques.

One of the attractions of snooker is that no two frames are the same. Each one is likely to present a different set of problems from the last. It would be an easy game to play if every shot could be made as described in the last section, with a perfect stance, a perfect bridge and all the room you needed to do exactly what you wanted. But the cue ball has a nasty habit of finishing in awkward places – and of course your opponent is deliberately trying to put the cue ball in such places.

I think one of the most difficult shots to play is the one when the cue ball comes to rest in a crowd of balls, or perhaps touching another ball in a way that prevents you striking the cue ball in the normal way. The ordinary bridge is out, and so are some of the requirements of a good bridge that I described as necessary. This is a situation where the position of the balls dictates your technique, and you have to adapt and accommodate. This doesn't mean that technique goes out of the window; indeed it means that you must be even more aware of good principles to avoid making an error.

Raising the hand from the table
Where a number of balls surround the cue ball, the bridging hand must obviously be placed where there's room for it. The closer the intervening ball to the cue ball, the closer the bridge will need to be. Sometimes your bridging hand will have to be over one ball while you cue over another, and the first requirement is clearly to place your fingers carefully between the balls so as not to 'foul' them.

The first thing is to get the bridge as high as possible. This requires the base of the hand to be raised from the table, thus removing one of the points of contact which give the stance its firmness. Maintaining stability is one of the problems of using a high bridge.

It follows that the fingers take even more responsibility than with the normal bridge. They must be well splayed, and there must be plenty of pressure on the fingertips – so much pressure, in fact, that the fingers are bent inwards to get as much of the pads onto the table as possible.

The thumb is cocked as high as it will comfortably go. According to the lengths of your fingers, this could bring the 'v' through which the cue travels as much as 4 inches (10cm) higher than the table, and all of this will be needed. In a really awkward situation, perhaps with two or three balls blocking access to the cue ball, the bridge might need to go even higher. The only thing you can do is to push the wrist forward, and raise it so that it follows the line of the fingers, all being nearly vertical. This will

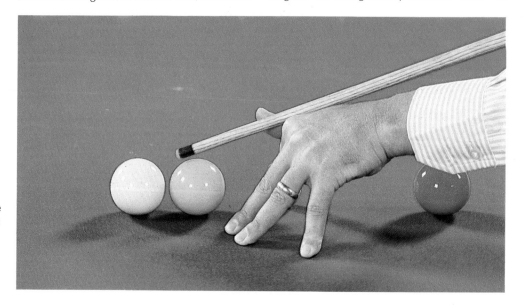

Cueing over an intervening ball. I have had to raise my bridge very high. Notice how the tips of the fingers are bent as I press them to the cloth for stability.

have the effect of lifting the little finger off the cloth, and perhaps the first finger too, and most of the pressure will be on the long middle finger. It's absolutely necessary in this case to be balanced and to concentrate on remaining steady.

The stance for a high bridge

When bridging over an intervening ball, it's obviously impossible to keep the cue horizontal – another of the requirements for a straightforward unhindered shot. The cue has to come downwards over the intervening ball, and will be able to strike the cue ball only near the top. Because of the raised cue, your head must be higher for sighting, so the stance is more upright.

The principles of a good stance apply as firmly, however. You must be comfortable, balanced and steady. The bridging arm should be rigid and straight, keeping those fingers pressed into the cloth. The cueing elbow will be higher than usual, but the principle that the line of cue should continue through wrist, elbow and shoulder is as important as ever.

The cueing action will be shorter and slower than usual. You cannot play a power shot under these conditions. Don't be ambitious. The fact that the cue is coming downwards onto the cue ball means that there can be no follow-through.

This fact leads to the most common fault among beginners not happy with having to play this shot. There is a fear of following through onto the cloth which leads to a scoop shot. The shot must be firm and confident, not a tentative stab. A tentative player is also inclined to try to leave the table

quickly, to get the shot over with, and consequently is not well balanced. Decide to stay in position after the shot, and you'll play it more confidently.

Sitting on the rail

Because of the upright stance, and the impossibility of stretching the bridging arm, shots requiring a high bridge can be played without a rest only when the ball is within, say, 2 feet (60cm) of the cushion. Sometimes a little extra height and reach can be obtained by sitting on the cushion rail. Remember to retain all the principles of the cueing action.

No doubt it is incorrect English to call sitting a stance, but whatever it is you are doing, be balanced and comfortable. And remember to keep one foot on the floor to avoid committing a foul.

With the red ball closer than in the previous picture, I have had to improvise this bridge. Notice the pressure on the little finger.

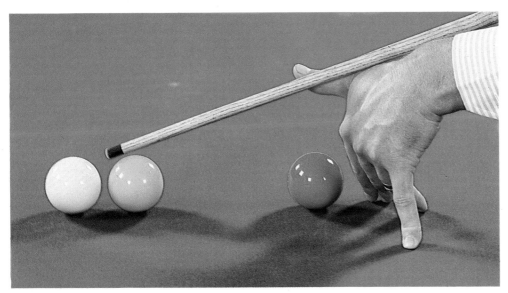

This is a bridge I use when I can't get close to the object ball. It is similar to that above but must be higher, so great care must be taken with its stability. The little finger is again pushing into the cloth.

CUEING UNDER THE CUSHION

‘ When the cue ball is against the cushion, there's not much of it visible to hit. This need not worry you if your technique is correct, but on the other hand you increase the chance of a miscue if your tip is shiny. Always make sure before you play these shots to chalk your cue. The surface of the cue ball slopes away from the tip, and the tip has a better chance of gripping if it is well chalked. ⟩

With the cue ball under the cushion, or for any shot where the cue ball is close to the cushion, shorten the cue. I am holding the cue here almost where the butt ends, i.e. close to the point of balance.

Opposite: Three ways of playing when the cue ball is near the cushion. *Top*: with a looped bridge; *centre*: with a normal 'v'; *bottom*: with the fingers gripping the front of the cushion.

Safety play is now so good in the professional game that I'm likely to have to play perhaps a dozen or more shots per frame with the cue ball within 12 inches (30cm) of the baulk cushion. This is another awkward cueing situation.

Some of these shots will be with the cue ball right against the cushion, allowing only the top of it to be struck, and this is very difficult to get right.

The stance and the general principles of the cueing action are not altered for these

shots. It is also possible, and desirable, to keep the cue horizontal, so the only amendments to the normal stroke come with the bridge.

In this section I'm assuming that I need to play up the table, i.e. more or less at right angles to the cushion.

If the cue ball is around 16 inches (40cm) or so from the cushion and clear, then there's room to place the bridging hand on the table normally.

It's possible to get the hand on the table if the cue ball is as close as 12 or 14 inches (30-35cm) to the cushion, but the bridge would be too close to the cue ball to allow a proper backswing, so you have to adapt. What I do is lay the wrist on the cushion itself, and raise the bridge slightly. The base of the hand and thumb has to come off the table, but the wrist supplies a substitute. It's

not so firm as the base of the hand, which makes the splayed fingers more important as a grip for firmness, but otherwise the bridge is not very different from the normal one.

When the cue ball is within about 10 inches (25cm) of the cushion, then the bridge comes off the table altogether. The fingers now grip the cushion at the front edge. The thumb is used quite differently. The cue is not supported in a 'v', but by the cushion. The forefinger comes over the cue, which runs between it and the middle finger.

The thumb is tucked inward under the first finger, and the cue brushes the thumb and first finger. They provide a sort of rail, but don't guide the cue.

I like to get my bridging hand slightly further back and might do this even if it lengthens the distance to the cue ball. This allows me to take my thumb out from under the forefinger and clamp it to the side of the table. The cue runs over the joint of the thumb.

With these shots it's important to remember that the cushion is used to support the cue. As the cushion is firm and will not wobble, these shots are not too difficult.

When the ball is 6 or 7 inches (15-20cm) from the cushion, the knuckles at the roots of the fingers will be at about the edge of the table. The fingers should be flat on the wood, with the tips (at least of the first three) on the cushion. The thumb is now free to form a 'v' with the first finger. The cue runs through the 'v' but is not supported by it; it runs across the top of the cushion.

It's also possible to play a ball near to the cushion with the looped bridge described in the next section.

Cue ball against the cushion

If the cue ball is tight to the cushion or very close to it, then I find the best bridge is with the wrist dropped so that the part of the palm of the hand which joins the fingers is pressed against the side of the table. The fingers are splayed and flat on the wood and the top joint of the thumb provides a 'v' with the forefinger. Grip the cue further up the butt and tighten the grip for more control.

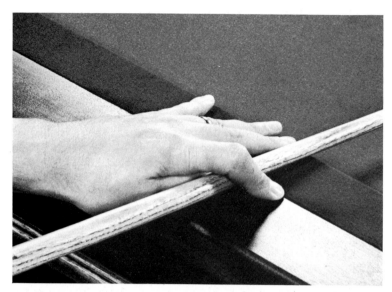

With the cue ball against the cushion only the top of it can be hit. The cue still brushes the edge of the cushion top, but the 'v' also supports the cue, which is raised very slightly above horizontal. By slightly I mean perhaps a couple of inches (5cm) in its length. The most common fault of beginners is to raise the cue too much in an attempt to dig down into the ball. It's an understandable effort to get more ball to hit, but it requires the knuckles to be raised and makes for a wobbly bridge and a possible miscue.

It's better to concentrate on keeping the cue horizontal. If you play the shot confidently and carefully there's enough of the ball to hit to make a proper shot.

If it's absolutely necessary for me to play a powerful shot with the cue ball against the cushion, I raise my bridge hand, but as the fingertips, which are pushing into the wooden rail rather than cloth, are the only support for the bridge, I realize that this is a risky shot. It is not one to attempt until you've mastered the basics.

Striking a cue ball which is tight against the cushion is so difficult that you should be aware of the danger of leaving it there in breakbuilding. Even professionals miss blacks off their spot because they have left the cue ball on the side cushion.

THORBURN'S TIP

● *It is interesting to note that of the approximately 72 square feet (6 square metres) of a snooker table, more than half is within 12 inches (30 cm) of a cushion. So, as the cue ball will often finish there, get used to incorporating the cushion into your bridge.*

PLAYING ALONG THE CUSHION

When using an awkward bridge, don't attempt an ambitious shot. Trying to use side often leads to trouble. Be content to play safely. The most important thing is to pot the object ball.

One bridge that can be used anywhere on the table, but is particularly useful for playing along the cushions, is the bridge where the forefinger forms a loop.

If the looped bridge is used in the centre of the table, the last three fingers are splayed and dug into the cloth, as usual. The forefinger, however, is looped over the cue, meeting the centre knuckle of the middle finger. The thumb is not cocked, but meets the tip of the forefinger, in effect forming the loop. The base of the palm, including the base of the thumb, is pressing firmly into the cloth.

The cue runs through the loop, along the thumb, and over the top of the middle finger. The thumb and finger forming the loop obviously do not hold the cue so firmly that there is resistance when you play the shot, but the bridge is firmer than the more popular 'v', and you might find it useful for 'forcing shots'.

Some players like to use this bridge for playing away from a cushion, when the ball is perhaps 12 inches (30cm) from the cushion, and to place the bridge on the cushion would give them more distance from bridge to cue ball than they like. In this instance the base of the palm is on the cushion, with the tips of the three fingers pressing into the cloth. The thumb and forefinger form the loop as before, and the

cue runs through the loop just above the cushion.

I find this form of bridge most useful, however, for those shots where the cue ball is very close to the left-hand cushion and I want to play up the table – parallel, or nearly so, to the cushion. I'm still assuming that you, like me, are right-handed – if not you can, of course, reverse the instructions.

The middle finger presses into the cloth of the bed of the table, while the two shorter fingers lie along the top of the cushion, again gripping for stability. The thumb and the forefinger form the loop as before. Sometimes it might be possible to place two fingers on the bed of the table.

The point about these bridges is that they are adaptable to the shot you wish to play. There isn't a 'correct' bridge for every shot. As long as you understand the function of the bridge, you form one which you find most convenient. You must be comfortable, balanced, not over-reaching, and forming a firm immovable platform for the cue.

When seeing the need for a shot to be played up the cushion, don't therefore automatically assume a looped bridge. If the cue ball is an inch (25mm) or so from the cushion you might find you cannot comfortably spread your hand wide enough to support the cue in a loop from the cushion. You would be advised to use your normal 'v'

Playing along the cushion I am here using a looped finger bridge with two fingers pressing into the cushion and the little finger along the rail.

bridge with the palm of the hand on the cushion, but with the first two fingers on the bed of the table and the other two flat on the cushion top or rail. The thumb can be cocked to form a 'v' as usual.

Playing along the right-hand cushion

Playing up the right-hand cushion is a different problem, because here the cushion is closer to your thumb and the cue. This shot is most difficult when the ball has to be played at a slight angle away from the cushion. The cue therefore doesn't run parallel to the cushion but cuts across it awkwardly. Here I adapt the bridge described in the previous section, with the thumb tucked in, but this time the small finger and its neighbour are the two pressing into the bed of the table, with the middle finger pressing into the side of the cushion. The first finger comes over the cue but without forming a loop with the thumb. Its tip presses into the top of the cushion. The thumb is tucked in under the first finger and provides the support for the cue. Note the first finger does not grip the cue, but merely provides a channel; the cue finds its own path.

With these shots along the cushion, it often helps to lay one leg along the edge of the table, enabling you to get closer to the shot. Remember the necessities of the actual stroke. The head must be over the cue, your stance must be firm, and the cue must come through in a straight line from the hinge at the elbow. And don't be in a hurry to get up: hold the position until the shot is completed as always.

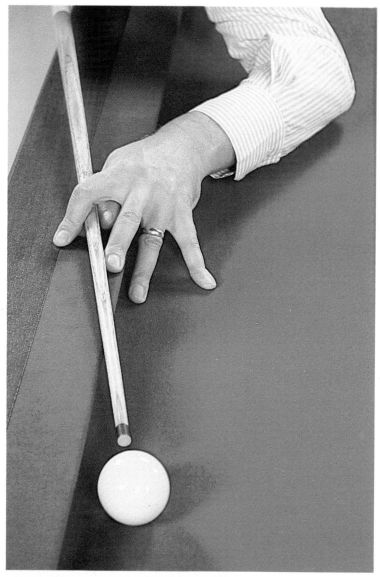

Above: Playing up the right-hand cushion, I can get two fingers onto the bed of the table and two on the cushion, providing a comfortable bridge.

Left: With this shot, played more parallel to the cushion than that opposite, I am gripping the inside of the cushion with two fingers, while still using a looped bridge.

USING RESTS

All players prefer not to have to use the rest, and some climb over the table and fold themselves into all sorts of shapes to avoid it. But sooner or later the rests must be used, so it's important to be confident when using them. Many players over-reach in their anxiety not to use a rest, and when they miss it saps their confidence. Far better to practise with the rests and use them naturally and without worry.

Occasions will arise when you can't reach the cue ball to form a bridge, and in these cases you need one of the rests available to you. I'm quite tall, and find that from the bottom of the table I can comfortably play the cue ball without a rest up to about 12 inches (30cm) short of the blue spot. Any further away and I think about using the rest.

The ordinary rest has a head in the shape of an 'x', though it may be more convenient to regard the head as four 'v's meeting in the middle. You will notice that one pair is deeper than the other. One 'v', of course, is to be used as a channel for the cue, so immediately you have to make a decision – high 'v' or low 'v'?

It's almost possible to say, 'always use the low 'v''. This is still higher than your bridging hand, and you won't be able to keep the cue horizontal, but it will be nearer horizontal than if you use the high one. The low 'v' allows you to make any shot. If you are so grooved in your action with the rest that you always use the cue at the same angle, and find that by using the high 'v' you can strike the cue ball higher when necessary without altering your angle, then I agree you have a good case for using it. But if this is the case you're already an expert.

The cueing action is quite different when using the rest. The head of the rest should be not more than 12 inches (30cm) from the cue ball. The rest should be at a slight angle to the line of shot, and resting on the table, with the left hand firmly holding it down. The head of the rest must not move, of course. It gives you and the rest stability if you can get your left elbow down on the table or cushion rail.

Not all top players hold the butt quite the same. I follow the most popular method which is to hold the butt an inch or two (2.5-5cm) from the end with the thumb supporting it underneath, the first and second fingers coming round over the top to grip it, and the other two fingers supporting at the side.

The action is, of course, quite different from the normal cueing action. It's a 'sideways' action of the right arm. The elbow sticks out to the right, and the wrist and forearm push the cue forwards. The fingers and thumb provide both power and control.

The sighting when using the rest is from a point above and behind the end of the butt, which is pointing more or less at the chin. You have the whole cue to sight along.

Feathering when using the rest is very important, and there will probably be side-to-side 'waggles' in the forward and

Using the standard rest. Notice the technique, which is almost like a 'backhand' push.

backward motion as you get the cue straight. Playing the shot is as before, with a backswing, very slight pause, then forward into the ball. Make sure you follow through, and don't rush to get the rest out of the way: stay with the shot.

The long rest

Using the ordinary rest from the baulk end, I can reach a cue ball just short of the pink. To reach any further, I need the long rest, or half-butt. This is about 9 feet (3 metres) long, and is accompanied by a long cue. As I mentioned in the section on cues, I prefer to use an extension to my own cue with this long rest, as do most professionals.

When using the long cue, always check first that it is chalked properly. Notice that it has a bigger and thicker tip than the ordinary cue. Never try anything ambitious when using the half-butt: it is a very difficult implement. The principles of shot-making are the same as with the ordinary rest.

Spiders and swan-necks

Of course the problem of intervening balls is just as likely to arise when you are forced to use the rest. You will need the 'spider' rest.

This is another difficult rest to use, because you are cueing down over a ball with only the top of the cue ball to hit. Playing a shot with a high bridge formed by the hand is hard enough, but with the spider you are playing it from a distance.

The secret is to hit the cue ball as low as you can and to play smoothly, i.e. not to jerk the shot. The tendency is to be afraid of

fouling the intervening ball, and to jerk the cue out of the way. Once again, stay with the shot.

If there are a number of intervening balls then you will need the extended spider. This rest will be mostly used early in the game, when the cue ball has been left among the pack of reds, with one of them 'on' into a corner if only you can get at the cue ball. All the previous principles apply to playing the shot – and particularly the one about not being ambitious.

A new and useful rest is the swan-neck. The business end of the cue can be extended and made to point in any direction, so it's not unlike the popular brand of lager: it can reach cue balls that other rests cannot reach.

Using the spider. The stance is upright but the cueing action is similar to that of the two other photographs on these pages.

I remember gambling with Paul Thornley, the former Canadian snooker champion, in Toronto – with 60 start I had to use a rest on every shot, even those from the bottom cushion. Once I made a century! We played 25 or 30 hours like this one week, and for a period which lasted for about six months afterwards I must have been about the best player with a rest in the world.

Using the standard rest for a shot which I can reach only with my cue extension. I am leaning more over the table than in the photograph opposite and have had to take my left leg out of the way.

SPIN

❛ Don't be seduced by the attractions of spin before you can play all the plain ball shots. You'll do better playing plain ball shots well than by using spin badly. And remember that however well you can control the cue ball, it's the other ball that is called the object ball, and the first object is to pot it. ❜

So far we have considered striking the cue ball in the centre, known as a plain-ball shot. Unfortunately you will rarely make breaks of more than 30 or so, no matter how good a player you are, without the mastery of the cue ball which comes from using spin. By striking the cue ball off-centre, you can impart spin which makes the cue ball behave differently on impact with the object ball and the cushions. In certain circumstances it's possible to choose where to leave the cue ball in quite a large area. This of course makes the next shot so much easier, and a mastery of spin makes those longer breaks possible.

Having said that, I must emphasize that there's little point in attempting to use spin before the basics already discussed in this book are mastered.

Imagine the blue ball on its spot, and the cue ball 12 inches (30cm) to the side, in a direct line with the centre pocket. If you

played an ordinary plain-ball pot into the centre pocket, at slow to medium pace and striking the cue ball at the centre, the cue ball would follow the path of the blue and stop, say, half-way to the pocket.

If you then played the same stroke but struck the cue ball at the top, the cue ball would be spinning forwards, and after contact with the blue would follow the blue further, and you could make it follow it into the pocket. This is called *topspin*.

If you played the same stroke but struck the cue ball at the bottom, the cue ball (despite travelling forwards) would be spinning backwards, and after striking the blue would come backwards along its path. You could bring it right back to fall into the opposite pocket. This is called *screw*. A shot played to bring the ball back a long way, and therefore played quite powerfully, is called a *deep screw*.

It follows that by judging the amount of

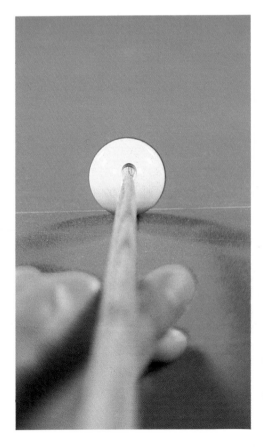

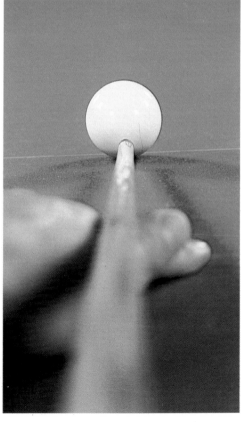

My view of the cue ball as I impart three types of spin. *Left*: top spin; *centre*: screw; and *right*: left-hand side.

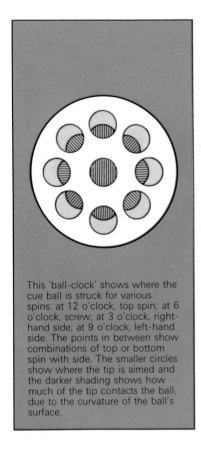

This 'ball-clock' shows where the cue ball is struck for various spins: at 12 o'clock, top spin; at 6 o'clock, screw; at 3 o'clock, right-hand side; at 9 o'clock, left-hand side. The points in between show combinations of top or bottom spin with side. The smaller circles show where the tip is aimed and the darker shading shows how much of the tip contacts the ball, due to the curvature of the ball's surface.

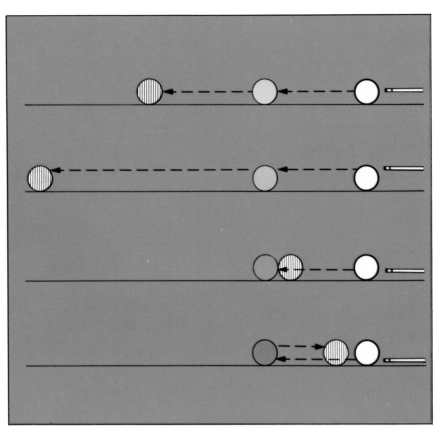

topspin or screw you apply, you can pot the blue and stop the cue ball at any point between the two centre pockets. If you strike the cue ball just below centre, so that the backspin isn't enough to bring the cue ball back, but enough to stop it dead, that is called *stun*. Actually this particular example is called a *stun dead*. Most pots are at an angle, when stun stops the ball travelling far, rather than stopping it dead.

However, it's when the contact with the object ball is not full ball, but at an angle, that spin comes into its own. Here, playing the ball with topspin or screw will not only alter the angle at which the cue ball leaves the object ball, but also the distance it will travel.

Side is the striking of the cue ball at either the right or left side, i.e. at 3 o'clock or 9 o'clock. It doesn't affect the angle at which the cue ball leaves the object ball that much, but is most useful when used in conjunction with a cushion. Side is very complicated, and is discussed more fully later (see page 46). Clearly, there is an infinite number of spots round the cue ball where the cue can strike it, and this enables the top players to put the cue ball almost where they want. It's safe to say that nobody has made a century break without such cue ball control.

The effects of top spin and screw. The cue ball hitting the yellow is struck centrally, and will continue on its path to the point shown. The cue ball hitting the blue is struck with top spin, and will follow further, as shown. The cue ball hitting the red is struck just below centre, the slight backspin causing it to stop dead, while the cue ball hitting the brown is struck with bottom spin and will screw back as shown.

SCREW

All spin shots are helped by a good table with a good nap. The spin can only work if it can grip the cloth, so do not be disheartened if you usually play on a worn table and find difficulty in employing spin on it.

It's also necessary for the cue to grip the cue ball to impart spin, and here there is something you can do about it: make sure your tip is well domed and well chalked.

When playing a screw shot, the cue must strike the cue ball low down, but the principle of keeping the cue as horizontal as possible still applies. The main fault of untutored players trying to play screw is that they lift the butt of the cue and play down on the cue ball – and, frightened of splitting the cloth, they strike the cue ball much higher than they wish or than they think they do.

To keep the cue ball horizontal it's necessary to lower the bridge. This is achieved by turning the hand over, with the thumb lying on the cloth for almost its whole length. The weight is transferred towards the thumb, and is mainly on the pad at the base of the thumb. The fingers still grip the cloth, although not much grip remains in the little finger. The secret is not to lower the knuckles but to turn the hand. Some players switch to a loop bridge for a screw shot, but I see no reason to, except perhaps for a very deep screw. The action is as normal.

After years of experience, however, I think a player develops a 'feel' for the screw shot. It's a question of sensing the grip of the cue on the cue ball and helping it to impart the spin. I confess I don't know how to convey that feeling to another player, and perhaps it's a sort of illusion. My advice is to appreciate the principle of what's happening and to imagine the spin being imparted to the cue ball. In other words, as I mentioned in an earlier section, picture the shot in all its aspects. At the same time, play the shot normally, and see if in time you discover this 'feel' for yourself. Do not, on any account, try to invent a special flamboyant style for screw shots – you will get in deep trouble.

Effect of screw

When you make a half-ball pot, striking the cue ball dead centre, you will know by now the angle at which the cue ball travels after impact with the object ball. Try the same shot while applying screw and note the angle the cue ball now takes. Experiment by playing screw while potting the object ball from nearly full-ball to fine cut, and note the effects. Notice that the thinner the contact with the object ball, the more difficult it is for the backspin to take effect, as clearly the contact area with the object ball is less. In fact the cue ball will travel forward at first

When using bottom spin, the distance between the cue ball and object ball affects the amount of backspin that will be generated. Each cue ball is struck with the same strength. At 12 inches (30cm), the cue ball might screw back beyond its original position. At 2 feet (60cm), it might screw back, but not so far. At 3 feet (90cm), the effect might be to stun the cue ball dead. At 4 feet (120cm), the backspin might wear off altogether, and the cue ball run on in the drag effect (see page 45).

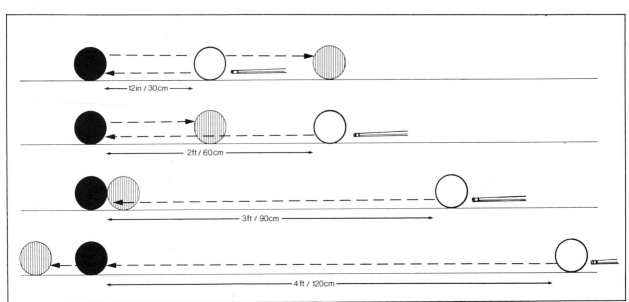

| 12 in / 30 cm |
| 2 ft / 60 cm |
| 3 ft / 90 cm |
| 4 ft / 120 cm |

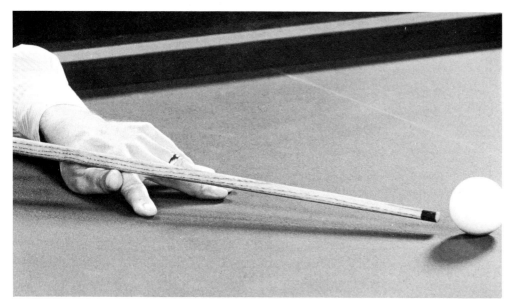

The bridge from three angles – the bridge for the screw shot must be lowered as explained in the text.

and then curve slightly as the backspin begins to work.

A deep screw merely describes a screw shot where the cue ball has been brought back a long way. This is achieved not so much by power as by the extra spin induced by striking the cue ball at the lowest possible point. It is for this shot that I use a loop bridge, but the usual principles apply in the shot. Because the cue ball is going to come back quickly, don't panic to get out of its way; follow through properly.

Screw shots are easiest to play and most effective when the cue ball is near the object ball. This is because the further the cue ball travels, the more the effect of the backspin wears off. We will see how to use this later.

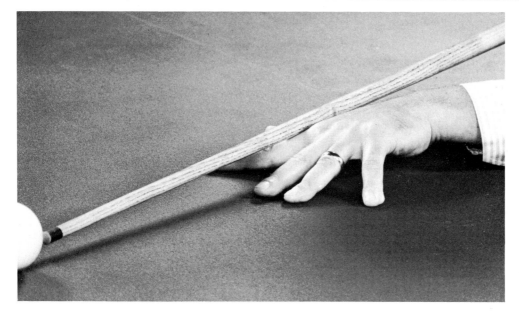

❛ When I first started playing – and even when I was North American champion – I used to raise my butt too high and I couldn't play screw shots too well. It took me a couple of years as a professional to sort this out – I didn't have a snooker book to help me. Don't make my mistake: keep your cue horizontal. **❜**

STUN

Stun is a term used very often in snooker, and it is the main weapon in the armoury of the player in his attempts to control the cue ball. Yet stun is not a separate shot from screw, for they both use backspin. You cannot even say that the difference between stun and screw is the amount of backspin, or where the ball is struck by the cue.

For example, imagine a cue ball and an object ball 18 inches (45cm) apart. You play a shot with the cue striking the ball low, imparting backspin, and the ball screws back towards its original position. This is a screw shot. Now imagine the balls 3 feet (90cm) apart, and you play exactly the same shot. Because of the greater distance the cue ball travels before impact, much of the backspin has gone. The cue ball strikes the object ball and stops dead. This is a stun shot.

The two shots were, in fact, the same. So the difference between a stun shot and a screw shot lies not in how you play the shot, but on its effect. A screw shot is one which brings the cue ball back; a stun shot, played in the same way, is one which impedes the forward progress of the ball. I deliberately don't say one which stops the ball dead,

because you'll frequently hear the expression 'stun-through'. This describes a shot where there's a controlled follow-through.

Distance between balls is not the only factor which determines the amount of backspin on contact. The speed of shot is another. A ball travelling slowly will lose its backspin more quickly.

Therefore there are three aspects to consider when applying backspin: length of shot, speed of shot and how low the cue ball is struck. Together, these will determine the behaviour of the cue ball, and whether the shot is called a screw or a stun shot.

Stun with run-through

The stun with run-through is a useful shot for running the cue ball through a short way after making a pot.

Without using stun, you would have to play the shot very slowly. This is always a dangerous procedure because it gives the ball an opportunity to deviate because of the nap. Very slow shots are always tricky, and with run-through stun, you merely strike the cue ball slightly higher than you would to stop it dead. This enables you to play the

I am potting a not quite straight pink and stunning the cue ball onto the black. *Left to right*: The first photograph shows the position, the second the moment after impact, the third the pink on its way to the pocket and the fourth the cue ball nicely on the black. Notice I have kept still throughout.

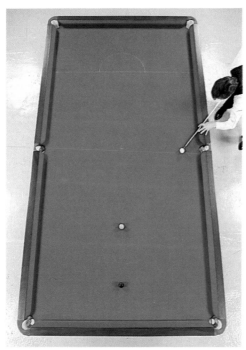
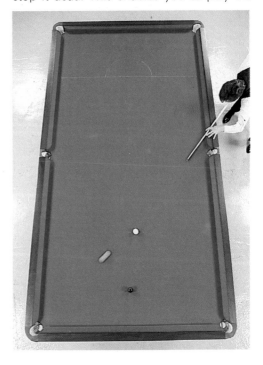

shot with more firmness, and you can make sure of the pot while still placing the cue ball where you want.

This shot came in very useful when I made my 147 break at The Crucible. I had a yellow to play into its baulk pocket, and would have left the cue ball near the cushion without using a lot of side. I played with stun run-through and came nicely onto the green. This was regarded as probably the best shot of the break.

Potting at an angle

If you're potting at an angle, you cannot stop the ball dead. But you can stun it, and indeed it's little stun shots around the black which are the basis of the very big breaks.

Suppose you have a three-quarter ball pot of the black into a corner pocket. By striking the cue ball at the place where you would stop it dead if the pot were straight, you will find the cue ball takes a path at about right angles to the path of the black to the pocket. But you can control how far it goes, and therefore keep the cue ball up among the reds.

You can, of course, control the angle of the cue ball to some extent, too, because you could use all variations from run-through stun to a screw. Provided you have a slight angle on the pot, you can place the cue ball anywhere in quite a large area.

As with all types of spin, the only way you can really learn the effect is to experiment and practise. Place the black on its spot, and

place the cue ball for a three-quarter ball pot. Play the pot at various speeds and with various amounts of backspin, and note each time the path the cue ball takes and how far it travels. It will help you to remember these effects if you actually have a plan of the snooker table and mark where the cue ball finishes for each amount of spin, trying to duplicate the effect. This will help you to keep an impression of these shots, whereas if you just play them one after the other you will have difficulty in spotting the pattern and logic of it.

The position for striking the cue ball for the shot in the sequence at the bottom of pages 42 and 43.

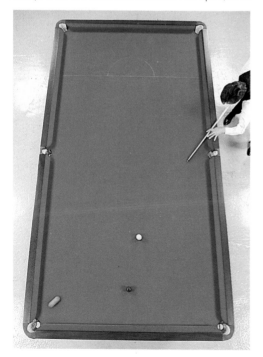

TOPSPIN

Topspin is used more in billiards than in snooker, where stun and screw are widely employed. But sometimes topspin is the only way you can achieve the position you want, and it should form part of your game.

The topspin shot is very useful, but not easy to play, because you are making contact with the cue ball with only part of the tip, just as you are for deep screw.

It's a useful shot if you have a fairly straight blue into a top pocket, say, and require the cue ball to follow through to leave you on a red. The straighter the shot the more resistance to follow-through there would be for a plain ball shot, so to get the ball to run you must impart topspin.

You must alter your bridge so that you strike the top of the cue ball with the cue horizontal. The way to do this is to draw back the fingertips about an inch (25mm) from their position for the normal bridge. With the base of the hand and thumb still pressing into the table, this automatically raises the knuckles. The thumb is cocked higher to form a 'v' with the higher forefinger. You must make sure you do not lose any stability by keeping the fingertips pressed into the cloth.

A common fault is to raise the butt end of the cue. The fear is obviously that with only the top of the cue ball to hit, there is a danger of the cue sliding over the top for a miscue, so the tentative player subconsciously digs down. This, of course, produces the wrong effect. The best way to ensure that the cue does not slide off the ball is to keep the tip in good condition and well chalked.

Practise by placing the blue and black balls on their spots and potting the blue straight into the top corner while running through for the black. Repeat the shot with a slight angle on the blue. Then position the blue half way between its own spot and the brown spot and repeat the exercise with the cue ball in various positions in the 'D'.

Another good practice is to place the blue on its spot with the cue ball 12 inches (30cm) away so that the pot is straight into the middle pocket. Pot the blue and make the cue ball follow it into the pocket. Move the cue ball back 6 inches (15cm) at a time as you master this shot, until you can play it almost from the jaws of the opposite pocket.

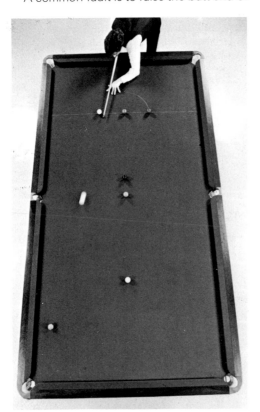 

I am 34 points down, so need the black with this last red to win with all the colours. I have struck the cue ball with top spin, and in the second photograph it has returned off the top cushion perfectly for the black.

DRAG

The drag shot is based on a similar principle to the stun follow-through, but the term is reserved for a shot where the cue ball travels a long distance. In professional snooker you often find a drag shot is used to pot the first red. It's employed when there's a long distance between the cue ball and object ball and you want to play the object ball softly.

An obvious situation is when, during the safety play at the beginning of a frame, your opponent has brought the cue ball back to near the baulk cushion, but has left a red invitingly near the pocket, say a three-quarter ball pot. If you can pot the red softly enough for the cue ball to hit the top cushion and come back by only 18 inches (45cm), you will be on the black with every prospect of a good break.

The problem is that to play the shot at a comfortable speed will bring the cue ball back too far, and to play the shot softly risks the cue ball drifting on the nap and the pot being missed. This will almost certainly present the chance of the big initial break to your opponent.

The answer is the drag shot, which is a sort of screw shot. You lower your bridge and strike the ball low to impart backspin, as described earlier. You can play the shot with medium power, but with the cue ball travelling perhaps 10 or 11 feet (300-330cm) before meeting the object ball, the backspin begins to work on it and slows it down before it makes contact. By then the backspin has worn off, and the effect at the other end of the table is as if you had played a soft plain-ball shoot from much closer range. Because you've been able to hit the ball much harder, however, it's less likely that the ball will deviate from a true line on its path up the table.

This is another example of the effect of a shot giving it its name, rather than how the shot is executed. What would have been a screw shot had the object ball been a foot away becomes a drag shot if the object ball is 10 feet (300cm) away.

The drag shot has been recognized as a useful shot for many years. The fact that spin will wear off if the cue ball travels a long way is used to control the cue ball while making the long pot easier.

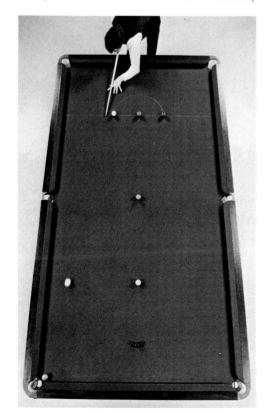

As on page 44, I need the black again, which this time is on its spot. This is a perfect set-up for the drag shot, and I have finished just right, on the black again.

SIDE

The top players in the world all have a tempo – a favourite speed to pot the balls. This is the speed at which it is easiest to play with side. If you have to play a shot with side which is either softer or harder than the speed you like, you must take even more care than usual.

Side is a very difficult subject. I don't think that the full potential of side has yet been exploited in snooker, and I also believe that many professional players aren't certain of the effects of side in every situation. I know you can reach a good club level in snooker without using side.

I am sure that nobody should attempt to use side until they are proficient in all the shots so far described in this book. While it's true that you won't be able to compete in the professional ranks without using side, I would say that you should be able to make your 25-30 breaks before you begin to worry about developing this aspect of the game.

Side is used to alter the angle at which the cue ball will come off a cushion, either before or after striking the object ball.

Without considering at this stage the various combinations of side with topspin or screw, side can be obtained by striking the cue ball at 3 o'clock (for right-hand side) and 9 o'clock (for left-hand side).

The cue should be horizontal as usual, so no alteration to the basic bridge is necessary. However, when playing with right-hand side, say, it's no use getting down as if you were going to play a plain-ball shot, and then to adjust your aim by pointing the tip to the right of the cue ball. You can see what happens if you do – the cue is now slightly out of line with the line of shot. It's necessary to keep the cue parallel with the line of shot. In effect, this means that to play right-hand side, your whole stance must be moved over by just over $\frac{1}{2}$ inch (1cm) or so.

The curve that side imparts

The first thing to notice when playing side is that the cue ball does not travel in a straight line. This is something new, because at least when you experimented with screw and stun the cue ball approached the object ball in a straight line, whatever it did afterwards.

If you apply right-hand side, the first effect is to push the cue ball to the left, and it then swerves back as the spin takes effect.

Make yourself familiar with this effect by placing the cue ball on the brown spot and aim firmly at the centre of the top cushion, using right-hand side. You will notice the cue ball begins by going fairly sharply to the left and begins to curve back somewhere around the blue spot, which it will pass well to the left. It will probably pass the pink spot on the left, too, although cutting across, and may pass over the black spot to make contact with the top cushion perhaps to the right of centre. The exact curve the ball will follow, and where it hits the cushion, will depend on how much side you put on the ball and on how hard you strike it. The harder you strike the ball, the longer it will take for the spin to take effect. The nap of the cloth is what the cue ball grips, so this, too, will have an effect on the two-way swerve. If you keep practising, you will soon see how this swerving effect works.

The next thing to observe is the angle at which the cue ball leaves the top cushion, and this is important because this angle is the very purpose of using side. It will leave the top cushion at a sharp angle to the right.

Playing the ball up the table with left-hand side (left) and right-hand side. The ball swerves in one direction and then curves back more gently. On hitting the top cushion it will break to the side. The paths of the cue balls are exaggerated, of course.

Playing down the table

If that seems reasonably straightforward, a complication is added when you play side *down* the table. Here the nap of the cloth affects the path of the ball in a different way. The ball played with right-hand side will deviate immediately to the left, as before, but at the point where, in the other direction, the spin begins to take effect, the nap of the cloth will not now allow the cue ball to swerve back. In fact it will continue to drift away.

You must practise this effect, too, but it's no secret that even professionals find it impossible to predict the exact path of the cue ball in these circumstances.

The consolation from this is that one rarely wants to play side at a distance of the whole table – indeed doing so is a real gamble. At short distances the effect of the nap of the cloth is less marked.

Potting while using side

Normally you play with side when potting in order to get an angle for the next shot, but the side makes the actual pot more difficult. To start with, as you have discovered, at no point is the cue ball travelling on the straight line between cue ball and object ball. It

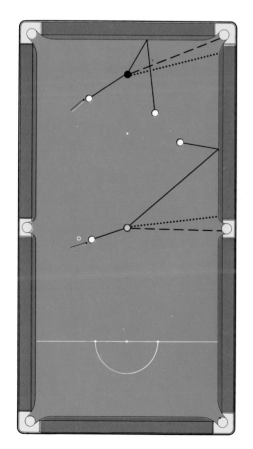

follows that when contact is made it will be at a slightly different angle from the straight one, so allowance must be made for this difference.

There's another effect when cue ball and object ball meet. The object ball leaves in a different direction from that anticipated. Again experiment will provide the key. Put the black on its spot and the cue ball to the left of the pink spot to make a half-ball pot into the right-hand top pocket. Play the pot with right-hand side. You will find that the object ball goes to the left of the pocket, i.e. on the top cushion side. Play the pot with left-hand side and the ball will go to the right-hand side of the pocket, i.e. to the side cushion. When making pots, you will have to allow for this effect.

Practise playing these pots at other angles to improve your technique and see the various effects of side.

Above: When playing with side, the cue must be kept parallel to the line of shot.

Left: When potting and using side, the aim must be adjusted. Potting the black illustrated with left-hand side, the aim must be just below the pocket. Potting the blue with right-hand side, the aim must be just above.

PRACTISING SIDE

'A friend of mine Robert Winsor, who as a 40-break player I thought was not ready to play with side, insisted I should teach him how to use it. He didn't find it easy and after a while I was accused of confusing him and ruining his confidence. Then he spoke to John Pulman, who advised him not to use side until he could hit 'centre ball'. Robert then began to pot balls from all angles. John got the credit for that – I still get the blame for nearly spoiling his game altogether. But fortunately we're still friends. '

We've seen how side changes the angle of the cue ball off the cushion. Since I believe that to picture something happening is an aid to making it happen, let's consider why this should be so.

Place the cue ball on the brown spot again and aim for the centre of the top cushion, using right-hand side. Now imagine the direction of the spin as the ball goes up the table. Looking at the ball from the position of the lights above the table, the ball is spinning anti-clockwise.

Now freeze the ball at the moment of impact with the top cushion: it's spinning anti-clockwise. With no other power, it would be running along the cushion to the top right-hand pocket. However, unfreeze the ball, and there is the power with which you hit it, which is going to make it bounce off the cushion and return back down the table.

The actual path the cue ball will take off the cushion is a compromise between this bounce back and the spin taking it right.

A ball hit with left-hand side will be spinning clockwise (from the top) as it hits the top cushion, which will push it to the left on its return.

A good practice to familiarize yourself with this effect, and to judge how much side you are imparting, is to place two object balls on the table, one in each of the jaws of the baulk pockets. Now play the cue ball straight up the table from the brown with side, first right and then left, to pot these two balls.

I hope that you do not have too much difficulty mastering those pots, because the next two are more difficult. Place the two red object balls on the edge of the middle pockets. Now from the brown spot play straight up the table and pot each of them.

In this practice, you must put more side on to the cue ball than you did in the first practice. This doesn't mean that you'll have to align the cue so far to the edge of the cue ball that you might slide off it altogether. More side can be obtained by striking the

A good practice for side is to pot the black from the position shown and go down for the yellow. I have screwed the cue ball back to the near cushion and taken it down for the yellow with left-hand side.

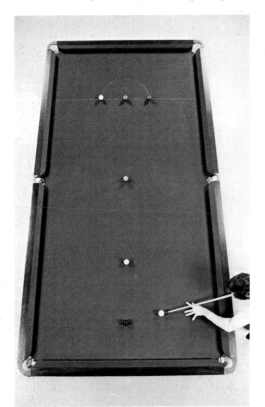
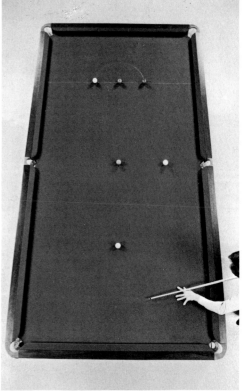

THORBURN'S TIPS

● *Don't regard side as a new and exciting plaything. Playing with side always makes a pot less certain than without it. So don't use side unnecessarily. If there's a choice of position, choose the plain-ball shot if all other things are equal.*
● *Side is most effective over short distances. When the cue ball travels most of the length of the table before making contact with a cushion, even professionals have difficulty in predicting its behaviour exactly.*

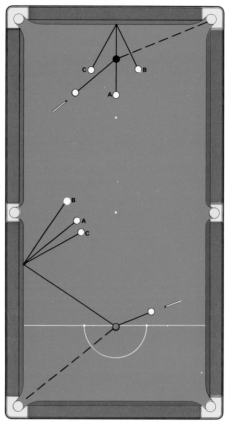

Half-ball pots of the black and the brown, showing where the cue ball might finish with centre-ball striking (A), running (right-hand) side (B), and check (left-hand) side (C).

cue ball lower. The tip must 'bite' on the ball. By now I hope I don't have to remind you of the value of a good tip and the use of chalk.

These practices are artificial, because it's very unlikely that pots like this will be required in a game. Shots like this are often needed to negotiate snookers, however, so try putting a number of reds along the side cushions, and from random positions in baulk hitting them by playing straight up the table with various degrees of side.

Negotiating snookers

A frequent use of side for avoiding snookers is when the ball on is near the top cushion hidden by perhaps a couple of other balls. Often you can play past the intervening balls to the top cushion, and by bringing the cue ball back at an angle with side, hit the ball that's on. Set up some practice situations for this and experiment. Since this situation is just as likely to arise with the ball on at the baulk end of the table, set up some snookers at that end too and play down the table at them. The curving effect of the ball will be absent (see page 47) but the angle of 'break' from the cushion will be just as great.

Running and check side

The main use of side is for the crucial short potting work near the black spot. Put the cue ball and the black 12 inches (30cm) from the top cushion, with the cue ball near the black spot and the black representing a three-quarter ball pot into the top left-hand pocket. First, play the pot plain ball and notice the angle of the cue ball after it strikes the left-hand cushion. Leave the ball where it finishes.

Replace the black, and with another cue ball (the yellow, say) play the pot with left-

hand side, at the same strength. When the cue ball hits the cushion the spin is helping it in its natural direction, and it leaves the cushion at a wide angle and with a slight acceleration. The cue ball travels well down the table. This is known as *running side*, for obvious reasons.

Now leave the cue ball where it is, replace the black and play a third cue ball, potting the black with right-hand side. This time the spin 'bites' into the cushion, and resists the natural path of the ball, which therefore leaves the cushion slowing down and at a narrow angle. This effect is known as *check side*.

If the pot is played into the right-hand top pocket, of course, it is right-hand side which imparts running side, and left-hand check side.

Notice the positions of the three cue balls in this experiment. Leave them where they are and use all the reds as cue balls, playing the pot with more or less side and at different speeds. You'll discover that merely by using side you can leave the cue ball in a wide choice of positions.

This is the skill which enables the top players to keep position in the big breaks, or to regain position after an error has led the cue ball astray.

POTTING ALONG THE CUSHION

‚ This is a specific shot where many players have found that using side helps them to pot the ball.

Whether or not the side spin on the cue ball is transmitted to the object ball is a question that snooker players have debated for years. There seem to be plenty of advocates on both sides.

My view is that the impact is so slight that if any spin is conveyed at all from one highly polished ball to the other it can only be of theoretical value, so the practical effect must be nil.

On the other hand, there is one shot where side definitely does help, and some players claim that it's because the side is transferred to the object ball.

The situation for the shot occurs when the object ball is tight against a cushion, and the cue ball is at an angle to it which affords a pot into the corner pocket at about half-ball or finer. This is a difficult shot at any time. It occurs frequently, however, particularly in relation to the black, which often finds its way to the top cushion.

One difficulty is that the angle of the pocket narrows the jaws, so the shot has to be precise, and another is that the object ball must run along the cushion – if it is bumped into it, the ball will come away and miss the pocket.

You can improve your chance of making this pot by aiming for a finer cut than you would expect, and if you are potting into the right-hand corner by playing with right-hand side.

There are three theories why this should be. One is that the right-hand side on the cue ball transfers to the object ball as left-hand side, causing it to hug the cushion. A second theory is that the wider angle at which the cue ball leaves the cushion keeps it in contact longer with the object ball and tends to force it to run along the cushion. The third theory is that the slight curve which the side imparts to the path of the cue ball means that it makes contact with the object ball at a slightly fuller angle (which is helped by the cue ball hitting the cushion first), making the pot in effect a fuller angle. I favour the last two theories more than the first one, and think they both contribute.

It's certain that the shot is more likely to succeed if played in the manner described, but it's still by no means a certainty.

With the object ball tight on the cushion, this is a very difficult pot, but prospects of getting it can be improved by using right-hand side. Nobody is certain why this should be.

THORBURN'S TIPS

● *The pot along the cushion is a very important one and you should practise it. How often do you see even at the top levels a break end because a black or a red has been played along the cushion and stayed out? The shot must usually be played slowly, and more often than not the ball stays in the jaws, and the miss can be doubly expensive. Any aid is welcome, so try the shot using side as explained.*

● *This is a shot where it is easy to work out your success ratio, as it takes only a matter of seconds to set up in practice. Keep a score of your successes and failures over a number of sessions.*

POWER SHOTS

Occasionally in a game a situation arises where you want to play a power shot. Perhaps the ball that's on is a fairly easy 'pot', but the only way you can get on the following ball is to take the cue ball round the table off four or five cushions. Or maybe you want to screw the cue ball back to baulk so that the pot is combined with safety.

Power shots look spectacular, but no professional uses them if there's another way. They are difficult to play, and if the easy pot is missed, you tend to feel silly.

The first requirement is of course to hit the ball hard. But there is no need to pile into the shot as if you were punching the heavy bag in the gym. It's essential to keep control and more of the power is generated by the crispness and timing of the shot than by sheer force.

You'll need a longer backswing for the power shot, withdrawing the tip right back to the bridge, and the forearm will have to come through quicker. The increased speed and distance is an opportunity for things to go wrong, mostly a loss of firmness in the stance. The cue wanders slightly from the intended path, and the cue ball is struck in the wrong place.

The first essential, then, is a controlled cue action with a solid stance. Resist the temptation to flourish the cue or lift the head to admire the ball crashing from cushion to cushion. If it's speed you need, aim carefully for the topspin. More power will come from striking the ball in exactly the right place than by hitting it harder while digging into it too low down. Remember the most important thing is the pot, and many pots are missed solely because power has been attempted.

The same basic principles apply if the power shot is a deep screw. Keep the head still and do not forget the follow-through.

One way of testing your power is to try a long shot from the green spot to just below the top right pocket, with strong side, so that the ball hits the top cushion near the pocket. See how much you can make the cue ball *throw*. Try potting a slightly off-straight black from 12 inches (30cm) behind it, and you should still get the same amount of throw.

Another way of testing your power is to use the exercise of playing the cue ball 'up the spots' to the centre of the top cushion. Start with the cue ball on the brown spot. If you can get the cue ball to go straight up and down and hit four cushions you're doing well, and will never need to play a more powerful shot in a game.

If the cue ball, when it eventually comes to rest, is still on the straight line over the spots, then you have indeed mastered the shot.

Spectators like to see power shots. Object balls thudding into pockets and cue balls swerving all round (or even off) the table are sights they enjoy. It is very satisfying to play a successful power shot.

Even so, I must repeat, do think carefully before trying such shots in competition.

Do not play the shot for show, and always look to see if a simpler and safer alternative is on.

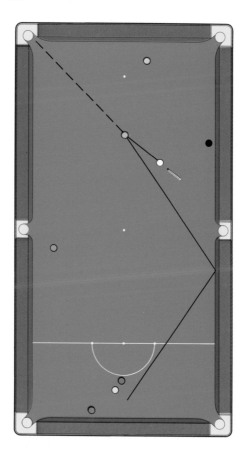

An example of a power shot – a deep screw on the pink to bring the cue ball down for the last red.

COMBINING SPIN

Topspin and screw, or backspin, enable you to control the cue ball in what you might call the backwards and forwards directions. But when you have an angle on the object ball, they also enable you to widen or narrow the angle at which the cue ball will leave the object ball, so you could say that they enable you to control the cue ball sideways as well. Side allows you to control the angle at which the cue ball will leave the cushion.

These types of spin need not be thought of in watertight compartments. Around the perimeter of the cue ball are an infinite number of spots on which the cue could make contact. Unless the cue strikes the ball on the direct line from 12 o'clock to 6 o'clock you will impart some degree of side, and unless it is on the direct line from 9 o'clock to 3 o'clock you will impart some degree of either forward or back spin. Anything in the sector around 4 or 5 o'clock is imparting both right-hand side *and* screw.

A combination of screw with side is often used in break-building. Combining spins makes for more difficult shots, of course, for there are more elements to go wrong. The amount of screw must be judged, the amount of side must be judged, the strength of the shot must be judged, and, of course, the pot has to be made.

Sometimes beginners get seduced by all this power at their fingertips, or cue tips, and play shots like this when almost the same position could be achieved using a simple stun shot.

Reverse effect of side after screw

In the diagram at the top of page 49, the effect of right- and left-hand side was seen when potting a brown off its spot into the green baulk pocket. Right-hand side caused the cue ball to run up the table after contacting the cushion, i.e. running side.

Right: The brown is potted with screw. If no side were used, the cue ball might end up at position A. Running side, to take the cue ball to position B, is left-hand side, while check side, to position C, is right-hand side.

Far right: The pot is a mirror image. Notice that right-hand side now produces running side (C), while left-hand side is now the check side. At the top the left-hand side used in potting the black will be running side if combined with screw (B), and check side if combined with top spin (C). The angles in the diagrams are exaggerated.

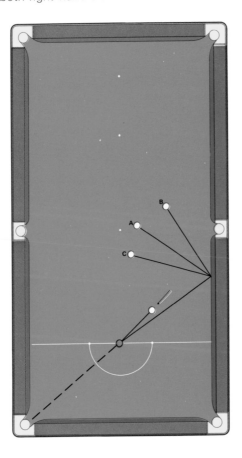

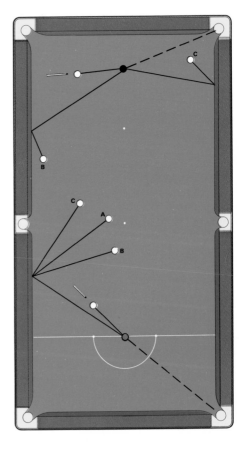

Now place the brown on its spot with a more or less straight pot into the same pocket, and pot it to screw back onto the side cushion, using right-hand side. You will find that the right-hand side now acts as check side, while you need left-hand side to get the ball to run up the table.

Combining side with topspin or screw is at its most useful around the black. If you can give yourself an angle to pot the black which represents a three-quarter ball contact you can gain position almost anywhere around the black spot for potting the next red into either top pocket. It's this fact which makes the building of a break seem almost inevitable when a top player gets an opening among well-split reds.

Side and screw around the blue

With prospects of a reasonable break on, a player will often find himself having to take a blue into a middle pocket, with the requirement of getting back up the table for the next red. The fuller the angle on the blue, the more difficult it is to take the cue ball up the table without using the cushion.

Place the blue on its spot, and the cue ball 12 inches (30cm) from it, but just below it, say on a line with the jaw of the right-hand centre pocket, so that the pot into the left-hand centre pocket is just off straight.

Without using the cushion, it's impossible to get the cue ball very far up the table with centre ball striking, but a combination of screw and left-hand side will manage it. The screw will bring the cue ball back to the cushion just above the right-hand centre pocket, and the side will then take it off the cushion in the direction of the pink spot.

Bringing the cue ball away from the cushion

A combination of screw and side can be used to bring the cue ball away from a cushion without using a cushion. Imagine you are potting a black, which is close to the left-hand cushion, into the top left-hand pocket (i.e. almost along the cushion). The cue ball is behind it, so that it is a straight pot, and you want to screw back, and at the same time bring the cue ball out towards the centre of the table. You can achieve this by using screw and right-hand side. Notice, however, that if you played the shot *against* the nap (i.e. a yellow into its pocket down the right-hand cushion – the right-hand, that is looking from baulk) you would need left-hand screw. This is because of the effect of the nap (see page 100).

Practice for combining spin

Place the yellow and green balls on their spots, and the cue ball just above the green, and practise potting the yellow with check side to bring the cue ball off the cushion to just above the yellow spot, so that you have a similar angle to pot the green.

Practise around the black by placing the black on its spot and the cue ball 12 inches (30cm) away, so that the black is a three-quarter pot into the top pocket. Then place a red anywhere within reasonable range. Pot the black and by any spin or combination of spin try to bring the cue ball to cannon gently against the red. The diagram gives you an indication of what is possible.

Try this with the red in different positions, and then alter the distance between the cue ball and black to see what effect this has. Then alter the angle of the pot to half-ball and see what constraints this brings.

When you think you can control the cue ball reasonably around the black, place the black on its spot and surround it with three or four reds. Then, placing the cue ball wherever you like to start, pot the black, gaining position on a red, then the respotted black, then another red, and so on to clear the table.

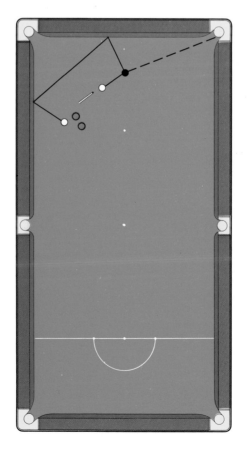

Using left-hand side and screw to pot the black and come off top and side cushions to get on a red into the top or centre pockets.

CONTROLLING THE CUE BALL

It must have become apparent by now that the control of the cue ball is of paramount importance in snooker. It's implicit in the term 'break-*building*', because to build a break you do not go from one haphazard pot to another; you plan ahead and try to place the cue ball where you can make the next pot easily.

If you cannot make a pot, cue ball control can enable you to snooker your opponent, or at the very worst present him with a difficult shot.

In the previous sections on spin we've seen numerous examples of how spin can enable you to make the cue ball leave the object ball in various directions and how you can use the cushions to help direct the cue ball.

However, there is far more to cue ball control than spin. Also important is *pace*.

Try this exercise. Place the yellow and black on their spots, and a red behind the black an inch (25mm) from the top cushion. The cue ball is just above the baulk line, 12 inches (30cm) away from the yellow towards the right cushion. Arrange it so that the pot of the yellow into the green baulk pocket is a half-ball pot.

You have to pot the yellow with enough screw to take the cue ball up close to the top cushion, to enable you to pot the red and get on the black. This is a test not only of your judgement in imparting the correct amount of screw, but also (and just as important), your judgement of the power and pace of the shot.

If you play the shot with excellent judgement, and the cue ball itself finishes an inch (25mm) from the top cushion, you will be faced with an interesting shot to get onto the black. It's worth practising in its own right.

Both object ball and cue ball are an inch (25mm) from the cushion, the object ball in

Right: Three-quarter ball pots of blue and brown showing the paths the cue ball might take if the object ball were potted with top-spin, with stun run-through and with deep screw.

Far right: Half-ball pots on the same colours make it impossible to get such a wide variety of angles. The angles illustrated are achieved with the same amount of spin as before.

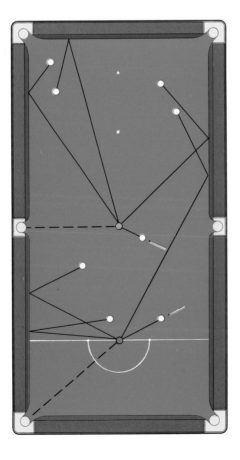

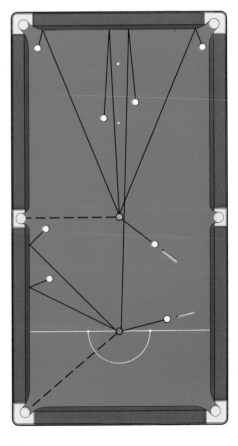

the centre, the cue ball 12 inches (30cm) to the right. The pot is not quite straight. You must play it with right-hand side and screw, so that the cue ball comes back to the side cushion just below the corner pocket, and then takes a wide angle to finish in position to pot the black. Here the screw, side and pace all have to be nicely judged and any miscalculation will make the black difficult.

Length of the table pace
Players and spectators new to snooker are always impressed by the accuracy with which professionals can judge the pace of the cue ball when they are playing gently into the pack off a cushion from baulk after a snooker, or, even more impressive, playing on to a red on the top cushion so that the cue ball just nestles against it.

They shouldn't be so surprised. According to the angle from the cushion, the ball might travel around 12 feet (3.6 metres). But it doesn't hit any obstacle on its way (except the cushion) and the good player should be able to judge the strength pretty well. You can practise this easily by placing a red on the top cushion and from behind the baulk line playing the cue ball off each side cushion, at various angles to rest against it.

The pace of the ball after contact
It's much more difficult to play the cue ball from near the baulk cushion up the table to contact a red, hit the top cushion and return to baulk. To get the cue ball to rest against the baulk cushion, as professionals do with regularity, takes some practice. As the ball doesn't travel straight up the table and back, and probably returns off a cushion, it might travel as much as 25 feet (7.5 metres). But it's the contact with a red that makes the shot so difficult.

If the red is hit at too fine a contact, the progress of the cue ball isn't checked as much as expected, and it comes back down the table too fast, to rebound from the baulk cushion. If the contact is too full, the cue ball will not return far enough, and could catch the angles of the centre pocket and go away.

Practise first by playing the cue ball from baulk up the table without hindrance to the top cushion, trying to get it back on the baulk cushion. When you can judge the pace accurately, place a red between the pink and black spots and try to do the same, but with a contact on the red. Move the red around, and try various paths back to the baulk cushion.

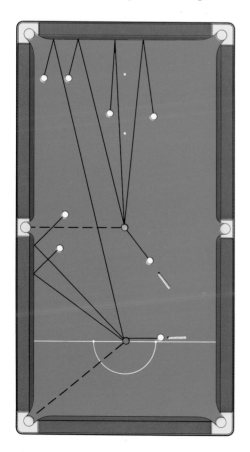
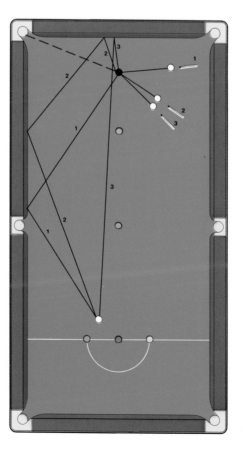

Far left: Continuing the sequence begun on the opposite page, quarter-ball pots restrict the angles available even more. Notice on the blue it is impossible to prevent the cue ball running towards the top cushion.

Left: Potting the black from half-ball angles (1 and 3) and from a three-quarter ball angle (2), it is possible in each case by stun run-through or top spin to bring the cue ball down for the yellow.

PLAY AROUND THE BLACK

We've already considered many of the special problems and opportunities of building breaks around the black. While there are plenty of reds on the table, and provided they are reasonably split, it's relatively easy to get on a red from the black.

With many positions, there will be a number of possible shots to play, and you must make a choice. I always select the simplest, and by this I usually mean the shot in which the cue ball travels the least distance. For example, suppose you're potting the black into the corner pocket, with the cue ball 12 inches (30cm) from the black and just below it, giving a three-quarter ball pot. There's a red half way between the pink and black spots that you wish to drop on to give you an angle into the opposite corner.

One way to play the shot is with a little topspin, to run through onto the side cushion, the natural angle bringing the cue ball back to a position 10 inches (25cm) or so from the red and below it, with a convenient three-quarter ball pot on to the opposite corner to get you nicely back on the black again.

A second way of playing the shot is to pot the black with sharp stun, the cue ball moving directly down the table to finish in exactly the same position as it did before.

The first shot is in some ways easier, as the spin is less, and the cue ball follows a more natural angle off the object ball. But I'd always choose the second shot. The reason is that the cue ball does not travel so far — only about 18 inches (45cm) — and I'm quite confident I can control it fairly precisely. The cue ball the other way travels nearly four times as far, and hits a cushion.

Furthermore, the shot I prefer guarantees a position on the side of the red that I want, whereas if I overhit the other shot I might pass it or, worse, finish directly below it.

Opposite: Do not be in too much of a hurry to decide on your shot. Here I am sizing up the situation in the 1985 Hofmeister World Doubles.

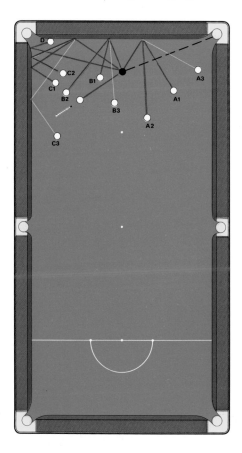
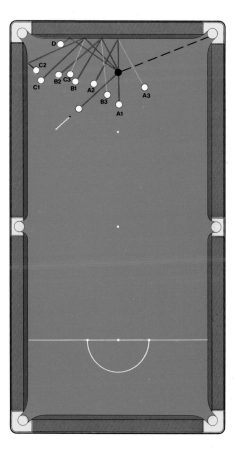

Far left: Paths the cue ball might take when potting a black with three-quarter ball contact. The paths lettered A are played without top spin or screw, those lettered B are played with stun, those lettered C with screw, that lettered D with deep screw. Paths numbered 1 (blue) are played without side, those numbered 2 (red) are played with left-hand (check) side and those numbered 3 (yellow) are played with right-hand (running) side.

Left: The same principles applied to a half-ball pot of the black.

SWERVE

When deciding whether to swerve or use the cushion in attempting to negotiate a snooker, bear in mind where the cue ball is likely to go in the event of failure and the consequences of a possible free ball.

The swerve shot is one you must master. Often there is no way to defeat a snooker other than by swerving the cue ball. Another situation where a swerve is particularly necessary is where a ball on (say a red) is over a top pocket, but you cannot get at it to pot it because of intervening balls. There's another red you could hit, but it would be difficult to cover up the red over the pocket, which would provide your opponent with an easy initial red and the probability of a frame-winning break. Your best option is to swerve round the intervening balls, hit the red, and, with luck, pot it. At worst, you will knock it from the cushion, with the chance of it going safe.

The swerve shot is played by imparting side in an exaggerated manner. We've seen how, when putting side on the cue ball, it swerves to one side before coming back. The problem is to make this swerve enough to go round a ball or balls while still controlling the cue ball. With practice, this can be achieved.

The exaggerated side is obtained by striking down on the cue ball, but first it's necessary to raise the bridge.

The palm of the hand leaves the table, leaving the bridge supported by the four fingers, all of which must press firmly into the table. The thumb is cocked high to form the 'v' for the cue.

Often the swerve shot has to be played from baulk, with the cue ball perhaps only 2 or 3 inches (5-8cm) from the cushion. In this case the bridge can be formed on top of the cushion, giving more height.

The cue ball is struck low down, either to the right or left, according to which way you want the ball to swerve.

In a swerve shot, a ball struck with right-hand side swerves very sharply to the left immediately, and comes back in a much more gentle arc. We studied this effect when we practised side (see page 46).

Raising the butt
To make the swerve pronounced, you must raise the cue butt. The higher you raise the

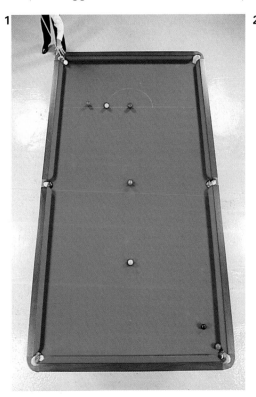

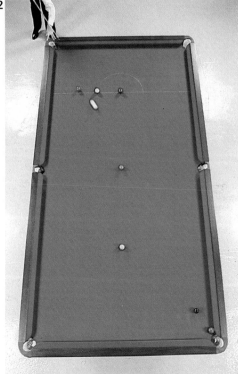

1-5: I am snookered on the last red by a line of green, blue and black. The only feasible shot is the swerve, which as you can see works perfectly, with the red potted.

butt, the more pronounced is the swerve.
When the butt is vertical we have the *massé*
shot, a very spectacular swerve indeed,
which follows on page 60.

The blow, then, is downward at an angle,
towards the bottom of the cue ball, so there
is very little follow-through. Any more
follow-through than half an inch (1 cm) and
the cue will strike the table. At the same time,
the shot cannot be tentative – the cue must
bite on the ball, almost driving it into the
table.

Surprisingly, this does not prove a
problem – with practice. Indeed, it's not
difficult to hit the cue ball too hard, so that
the ball goes out to one side as planned, but
the length of the table is not enough to bring
it back in its arc.

Picturing the shot

This is another occasion where picturing the
shot, and understanding what is happening,
helps you to play it. By playing down on the
ball, you're beginning its spin almost before
you are applying its forward motion. You
can, in fact, make it bounce slightly.
Therefore the ball starts with its spin forcing
its sideways motion. Then the forward
motion takes over, making the swerve back a
gentler curve.

It's easy to set up situations on the
practice table where you have to swerve

4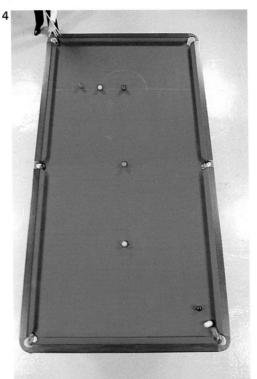

round a ball, or a clump or line of balls, to
contact the object ball.

Also practise shots against the nap, when
the ball behaves very differently (see
page 100).

3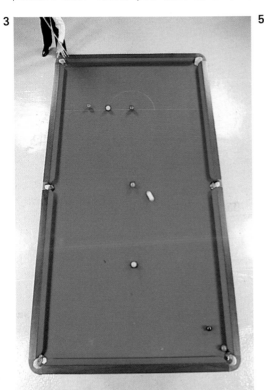

5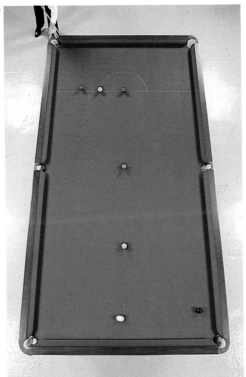

MASSÉ SHOT

❝ Not being a billards player, I have never really mastered the massé shot and always seek to play off the cushions rather than use it. It is a desperate situation if I decide to play a massé shot. **❞**

The massé shot is an exaggerated swerve shot played when a big swerve is required over a short distance. It's less necessary in snooker than in billiards, and there are many excellent snooker players who have never mastered it. Nevertheless it's a useful shot to have, and a satisfying one. In fact it's somewhat spectacular, and if you play one well the uninitiated will think you are a miracle worker.

It was said in the last section that the massé was the ultimate swerve shot, played with the cue almost vertical. However, this is easier said than done. In fact this so affects the stance, grip and bridge that really the massé shot is a one-off.

The first thing to be said is that it can only be played when the cue ball is close to the cushion. Obviously, with a near-vertical cue, nobody can lean over the table to sight down it if the cue ball is much more than 6 inches (15cm) or so from the cushion.

The stance is upright, but it still has to be firm of course. The shoulders are set firm. The cue is gripped further up the butt than usual; otherwise it's gripped normally.

The cue is nearly vertical. It does not touch the body, or the chin, cheek or ear as you

sight 'down' it.

The bridging arm cannot be rigid in this shot. It's bent, with the elbow tucked in, resting on the hip. This helps to keep the bridge itself steady. ·

It's in the bridge that the greatest difference between the normal shot and the massé occurs. The bridge is sometimes formed on the cushion top, sometimes on the table. The hand is upright, with three fingers forming the bridge. Since these three fingers are of different lengths, they obviously cannot be in line, and they form a tripod. They are pressed firmly into the cloth, and the wrist is arched, helping the stability of the bridge.

The bridge must be firm – any slight collapse of the bridge and you could miss the cue ball altogether.

Some players turn the palm of the bridging hand itself towards the centre of the table, practically side on to the cue ball. The forefinger is bent inwards, out of the way, and the thumb is bent to form the groove for the cue. The thumb is the only part of the bridging hand that the cue runs on. I like to keep the back of the hand more

Left to right: I am playing a massé shot round the black to pot the pink into the middle pocket.

towards the cue ball, as you can see. The 'v' is almost non-existent. Any mis-judgement in the cueing action, and the groove might be a notional one in mid-air. This is a complicated description, but I hope it helps you to get the right position to practise the shot.

Making the stroke

Having assumed this complicated posture, you make the stroke itself by striking downwards on the side of the ball, as if forcing it through the table. Needless to say, there's no follow-through.

Where you strike the cue ball governs how it will spin. If you strike it in the front, you will get topspin – the ball will momentarily go backwards and then shoot forwards as the spin grips the cloth. Struck at the back, the ball will do the opposite.

It is side, however, that is mostly required, since the massé is mostly used to swerve round an obstacle in a limited space. It might be used to negotiate a snooker, or to pot a ball on the jaws of a pocket. The swerve obeys the laws of the normal swerve shot, going at first sharply in the opposite direction before curving round more gently in the desired direction. 'Gently' here is used comparatively – in fact the swerve can be startling.

Whenever the distance between the cue ball and object ball is less than 6 feet (180cm) and the intervening ball is close to

the cue ball, a semi-massé shot is needed. At the distance of half the table it will be a gentle one – the butt will be raised high, but the cue will not be vertical. Where the two balls are only 12 inches (30cm) apart, the shot will be a forceful one. In billiards it used to be called a grand massé.

The only way of mastering the massé, and becoming familiar with the pace and swerve and niceties of the shot, is to practise it. You might use it in a match not more than once a year, but it's well worth mastering. Apart from anything else, a good massé shot does wonders for the confidence.

THORBURN'S TIP

● *In the professional game, it is not uncommon to see a player shape up to play a massé shot, but nine times out of ten he decides discretion is the better part of valour and chooses an alternative shot. Amateurs often try it, not always successfully. The massé can go very wrong, at which the player who attempted it looks foolish and could well lose his confidence. It is one shot which requires a lot of practice. If you want to use it in a match, first make sure that you can perform it on the practice table.*

❝ After I won the Canadian Open in 1974, which was the first big tournament in Canada with players from Britain, I was asked to do a commercial for a beer company. I chose to play a massé shot, and my friend Paul Rimstead placed one of the advertiser's beer bottles on the table so that I could pot the black by swerving round it. Having twice showed everybody exactly what I was going to do, perfectly, the crew set up the cameras and started rolling. My next 12 attempts missed. The point is that the massé is a shot you can often play for fun, but when the chips are down it gets a lot harder. I'm glad to say the commercial was eventually judged the third best of the year in North America. ❞

PLANTS

❝ A few years ago, television snooker commentators would refer to the plant as a 'speciality of the Canadian players', as if we'd invented it. It was regarded as something out of the ordinary. Nowadays, unfortunately, everybody plays plant shots, and if we had any advantage it's gone. I can't think why the plant shot should have become fashionable so recently because it's one of the safest shots in the game. ❞

The potting of balls by means of plants is a part of the game in which we Canadians have made a big impact. Strictly speaking a plant is the situation of two object balls touching each other in direct line with a pocket, such that by striking the first with the cue ball, the second will be potted. Nowadays the term is also used when there is a little distance between the balls, when it is said that the plant must be 'made'. I don't know if the term 'set' originally meant the first situation and 'plant' the second, but the terms now seem to be interchangeable, with plant getting the preference for all variations of the shot.

If the two object balls and the cue ball are all in line with the pocket, then there is no danger—the full-ball contact on the first object ball will send the second into the pocket. But if the cue ball is at an angle (as it usually is) then to be certain of the plant the first object ball has to be struck at the correct angle to pot it. Many players believe that striking the first object ball full-ball will ensure the plant. This is erroneous. Because the impact is not through the centres of all three balls, what is called a *squeeze* takes place between the balls, throwing the third ball slightly off line. You might say snooker balls once again defy geometry.

Of course this effect doesn't matter when the balls are close to the pocket, as the deviation is too slight to count. But to save yourself from the disappointment of missing a plant, aim as you would if you were attempting to pot the *first* object ball. Otherwise you will occasionally miss a plant, and believe that you misjudged it, and that it was not a true plant at all. It's more likely that the squeeze effect defeated you.

Of course, this effect can help you make plants that are not quite true ones. Place two reds near the pink spot so that they are pointing to the side cushion just below the left corner pocket. The cue ball is near the right hand cushion, just below the reds, making a half-ball potting angle.

This is not a true plant, but you can pot the second object ball by striking the first object ball finer, i.e. further to the left than you would to pot it. The squeeze effect throws the second ball to the right, and it's potted.

This in itself seems surprising, because you might think you should hit the first ball more to the right, so that it 'hits' the second cue ball to the left. But this is not true, as you can verify with practice.

Making the plant

Non-touching plants don't work this way at all, of course. In this case you are propelling the first object ball onto the second, so that in effect the first object ball acts as the cue ball. It must strike the second object ball at the angle to pot it normally. If, in the previous shot described, there had been an inch or two (25-50mm) between the balls, then, indeed, you would have needed to aim more to the right of the first object ball, to create the angle to pot the second.

Reverse plants

Reverse plants are possible when two balls are touching so that a line drawn through

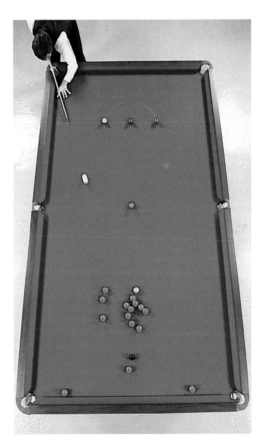

them is parallel to the jaws of the pocket. To be more precise, imagine a line drawn between the centres of the two balls. If an imaginary line at right angles to this line passing between the balls also runs to the centre of the pocket, then the first ball can be potted.

Set up two reds parallel to the side cushion, touching over the blue spot. Place the cue ball on the brown spot. By striking the first red well to the right, you will find it pots into the left centre pocket, and vice versa.

Situations like this can occur all round the table into any pocket, and need not concern only reds. If the nearer ball is the ball on, then it doesn't matter what colour the further ball is.

Practise by setting up all the situations mentioned in this section, and pot the ball on. If you miss some at first, you'll learn by experience, and soon be familiar with how touching balls behave when struck.

When playing, keep a sharp lookout for plants. They are among the easiest of shots once you know how to deal with them, and can frequently get you out of trouble. Nothing is more satisfying than to begin a break with a well-spotted plant.

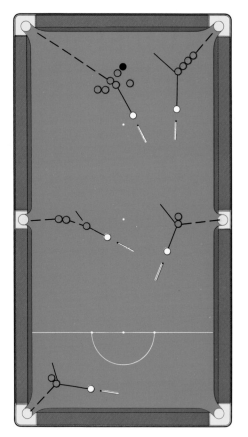

Examples of plants and reverse plants into various pockets around the table.

‘ When the balls in a plant are a few inches apart, I work out the contact I want the first object ball to make on the second object ball. Then I stand behind the first object ball and look along the path I want it to take. This enables me to line it up with something in the club or room I'm playing in, like a cue in a rack, the edge of a door or an empty seat. I can then play the shot on the first object ball as if I'm aiming it at what I lined it up with. I've got good peripheral vision and find this helps a lot – it might help you to try it. ,

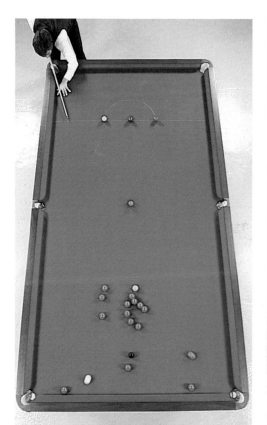

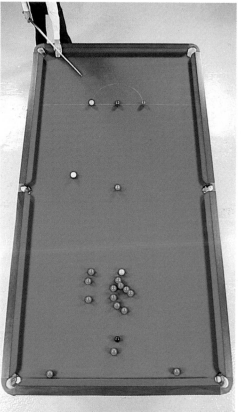

I have spotted from the baulk end that the two reds in the centre of the cluster might be a plant into the top pocket, and have gone to the top of the table to confirm it. *Far left*: I have played from just below the baulk line towards them; *centre left*: the red is on its way to the pocket; *left*: the cue ball has come down for the blue. This was not a shot to nothing, as I was confident of the pot, and played for the blue next.

DOUBLES

❛ It amazes me that players who think nothing of negotiating a snooker off three cushions are frightened of attempting a double off one. The double is a straightforward shot – as with any other, practice makes perfect.❜

A double is a shot which plays the object ball onto a cushion, so that it doubles back across the table and into an opposite pocket.

Most doubles are played into a middle pocket, since the middle pockets offer a wider target. Doubles into corner pockets are slightly more difficult, because the pockets are partly closed at the normal potting angles. The most common form of double is when the cue ball is somewhere around the pink spot, and the object ball is near a cushion, in such a position that a full-ball contact would send it onto the cushion and back across into the middle pocket. This is not a difficult shot.

Where doubles are not full-ball contacts, an additional calculation has to be made, which perhaps makes them discouraging for beginners. As well as the angle of contact between cue ball and object ball, the angle at which the object ball will leave the cushion must also be estimated.

It's difficult to teach in geometric terms the angles for doubles; they have to be learned by experience. There are three basic contacts of cue ball with object ball. First there is the full-ball contact, as already described. The second is the 'cut-back' double. Imagine the object ball 12 inches (30cm) below the left-hand centre pocket, close to the cushion, while the cue ball is near the blue spot. To double the object ball across into the other centre pocket, the cue ball strikes the object ball on the baulk side and travels towards the baulk cushion, while the object ball goes the other way.

The third contact is where the cue ball goes across the object ball after contact. If the object ball was in the same position as for the last shot, but the cue ball was near the yellow spot, then the path of the object ball would be the same, but the cue ball would proceed up the table. There is the danger here of the double kiss, i.e. the object ball and cue ball making a second contact after the former has hit the cushion.

Another double is called the 'cocked hat' double, and, while tricky, is not as difficult as it looks. The cue ball is below the pink spot, the object ball near the side cushion further up the table. The object ball is struck so that it leaves the side cushion and hits the top

cushion and the other side cushion before being potted into the centre pocket on the same side of the table as it started. The fact that the paths the ball takes when leaving the two side cushions are parallel helps you gauge the angle.

Doubles where the object ball is tight against the cushion are also tricky. It's difficult to judge the angle, and of course the cue ball is likely to interfere with the path of the object ball.

When playing a double into the middle pocket, particularly when it is a crucial stage of the match, like an attempt at the last red on the table, bear in mind that a miss by the nearer jaw will be more likely to send the object ball safe than a miss by hitting the far jaw, which will return the object ball towards you, and probably set it up for your opponent.

Many players play doubles with too much force. Presumably they are trying to guard against a narrow miss leaving their opponent an easy pot. I think this is false reasoning – apart from the fact that it's almost encouraging you to miss. If the ball travels 2 feet (60cm) away from the pocket it's as likely to be safe as if it travelled 6 feet (180cm).

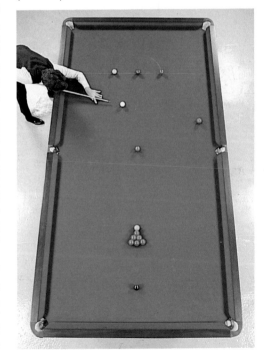

THORBURN'S TIPS

● *It's often said that professionals don't like playing doubles, but this isn't true. They would prefer the opportunity of a plain-ball pot, of course, but if the best shot available is a double, then they will play it. There's no mystery about a double. It's a useful shot to learn, just like the rest.*

● *No two tables are the same. If you are playing on a strange table and you miss a double, take note of which side of the pocket you missed. It may be that the state of the cushions contributed to the miss and that you need to make a slight adjustment next time.*

● *Look out for the possibility of doubling the ball off two cushions (would this be a 'treble'?) These are often scored by accident by a player missing the pot in the middle pocket intended, but seeing the ball go across the table into the other middle pocket.*

Another reason for not playing the shot too hard is the behaviour of the cushion. A ball striking the cushion hard tends to bury itself into the cushion and leave it at a slightly more square angle than it 'should'. And unless you play in the top championships you're likely to find cushions of varying quality.

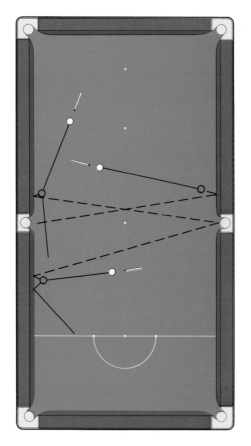

Examples of doubles. Doubles played into the centre pockets are much commoner than into corner pockets, since the middle pockets are more inviting at the angle the object ball takes.

Don't be afraid of doubles. A successful shot can transform a tricky situation into a match-winning one. So be prepared. Set up several doubles on the practice table and you'll soon become proficient at them.

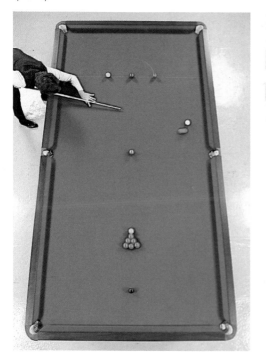

A straightforward double of a red into a middle pocket.

BREAKING OFF

At the top level, even in a long bout of safety play with no points being scored, one player is usually in the driving seat, setting the puzzles for his opponent to solve. He is likely to be the player who gets the first opportunity of making a break. The opening break frequently determines which player gets this early advantage, so make your first shot a good one.

In the professional game the opening shot is very important; in fact I think a good one is worth about two blacks start. If it's bungled, perhaps by contacting the blue with the intended return of the cue ball to baulk, then a frame can be virtually lost before you get another strike.

Many professional players, myself included, tackle the opening stroke in the same way. The cue ball is placed between the brown and yellow and struck to make half- to quarter-ball contact with the right-hand end red in the second row from the top. The ball is struck with running (right-hand) side, to widen the angle it takes from the top cushion, so that it comes off the right-hand side cushion and crosses the table just above the blue to hit the left-hand side cushion and end somewhere near, or preferably right on, the baulk cushion.

That's the preferred way, but some players have difficulty with this shot. They contact the end red of the third row, which tends to throw the cue ball in-off in the top right-hand pocket. So I suggest you take insurance by aiming to contact the end red in the top row, in exactly the same manner. This is also a perfectly good shot, which has the same effect so far as the cue ball is concerned, with no possibility of sliding in-off.

You should strike the cue ball slightly above centre, to avoid any 'drag' being put onto the cue ball.

The difference between the two strokes is that the first will split the reds a little more, which will be to your advantage if you can be sure of landing near the baulk cushion.

An alternative shot

Players who prefer to ease themselves into the game with a slightly more straight-forward shot can, from the same position between yellow and brown, play a plain-ball stroke to contact the end red of the top row at quarter-ball angle. This should bring the cue ball back off two cushions to pass to the right of the yellow on its way to baulk.

This shot has the merit that however much it's misjudged you're unlikely to hit the blue on the way back, but it carries its own dangers in that too full a contact would find the yellow or even brown in the way.

Opening break philosophy

The important thing in playing the opening break is not to regard it as a chore to get the game started, or a formality like kicking-off at football. When you have the opening break, you have the initiative. If you put your opponent in trouble, he might never be able to get back into the game.

Practising the opening break is admittedly tedious, because after every shot you have to rearrange the triangle of reds – but it is crucial.

All the shots mentioned could, of course, be played from the other side of the 'D', from between the brown and green. For some reason nearly all players break off from between brown and yellow. Before you get set in your ways it might be a good idea to practise from the other side. It could throw an opponent off his stride.

Many players don't like making the opening break, and if they win the toss they ask their opponent to break. Don't do this.

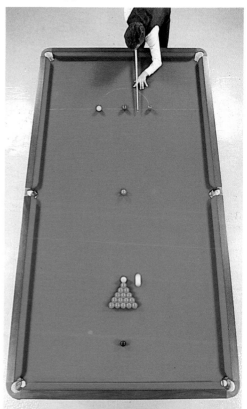

Practise the opening break until you're at home with it, and when you have the opportunity, break off confidently and seize the initiative.

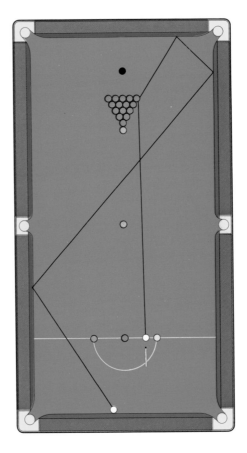

Breaking off by hitting the end red in the top row with right-hand side to take the cue ball across above the blue and onto the baulk cushion.

THORBURN'S TIP

● *One of the greats of Canadian snooker, Eddie Agha, could make the 'perfect' opening break. He struck the end red so that it went to the top cushion and back to its original place, while the red at the other end of the top row went to the side cushion and back to its place, so that the pyramid was perfectly formed again! This was not, of course, really a good shot – it meant, when I was playing him, that in effect he transferred the opening shot to me, and lost his advantage.*

The perfect shot is to leave the cue ball tight on the cushion behind the green or yellow, not snookering your opponent (he would merely roll into the pack off a cushion) but leaving him a red to hit, from which he must play a good safety shot or the advantage will be firmly yours.

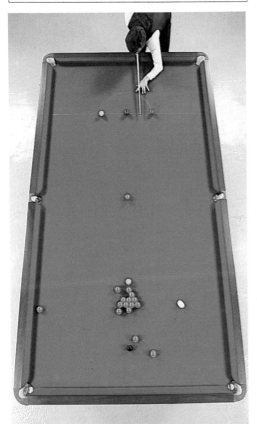

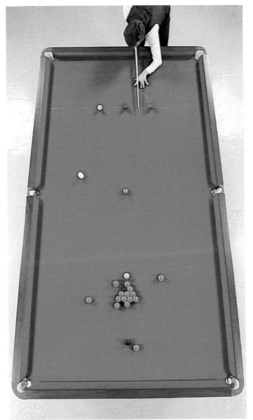

I am breaking off from between brown and green. I am aiming to hit the end red in the top row, and am using strong left-hand side, which brings the cue ball back between pink and blue to the bottom cushion.

PATH TO BAULK

After the opening break, the second player is probably looking at a more difficult problem than the opening player had; after all, he could place the cue ball where he wanted it within the 'D', while the second player might well be near the cushion. There could be two or three reds loose in positions which represent almost impossible pots from where he is, but if he makes a mistake they could well be on for his opponent. His first priority is to play the cue ball up the table, hit a red, and bring it back safely to baulk.

There are two ways of looking at this safety shot. Is it a good idea to break up the reds even more, and risk leaving one on, or should you try to disturb the reds as little as possible, putting your opponent in much the same position as you are now in?

The first option, splitting up the reds, might be called attacking safety play, if that is not a contradiction in terms, while the second option is defensive safety play.

Personally, I favour the more aggressive approach, but I suppose it's for each player to decide for himself. The game would be dull if we all played it in the same way.

It's certainly easier to sort out the best stroke if you favour the latter strategy. The usual way is to play a thin contact on a red which has become detached from the pack, coming off the top cushion and probably the side to bring the cue ball back to near where it was, at the same time possibly nudging the loose red back into the pack. The thinner the contact, the further the cue ball will travel in relation to the red. There's no danger of the red coming down the table with the cue ball.

The reason I prefer the other approach is that if both players are as cautious, this could go on for a long time! Sooner or later the reds are going to be split sufficiently for one player to try a pot, and there seems no reason why it should not be sooner rather than later.

Sometimes the difference between the

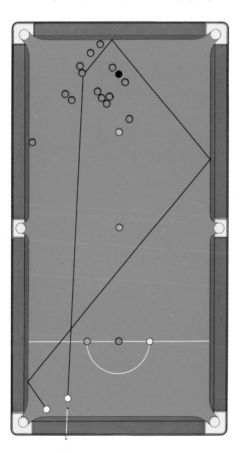

Right: A safe path to baulk, sending the cue ball round the back of the main cluster of reds and the black.

Far right: An aggressive safety shot. As there is no difficulty in getting the cue ball back to baulk, the opportunity can be taken to split the reds further, giving your opponent a more difficult task.

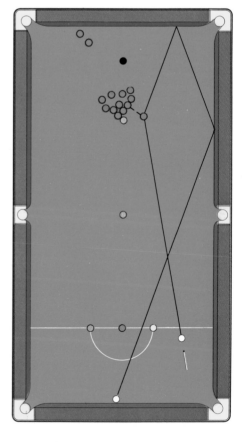

attacking and defensive strokes depends merely on how the same red is played. A red at the edge of the pack can be played thin, without spin, bringing the cue ball back down the same side of the table. On the other hand it could be played in the same way more forcefully with running side to bring the cue ball back across the table to the other end of baulk. This is useful when, as often happens, the reds get on one side of the table only.

What can go wrong

There are four main reasons why a player will fail to leave the cue ball safely in baulk as intended.

The first is that the ball will go in-off into a pocket, or else catch the jaws sufficiently to throw it off course. It could be a corner or middle pocket. If the ball catches the bump of the middle pocket and returns towards the black, it could be disastrous.

The second is that, in attempting to take the cue ball round the back of the pack, or between clusters of reds, the player will misjudge the angle and contact one of the reds.

The third is that he could get a double kiss, as when playing off a red near the side cushion, which could come off this cushion and meet the cue ball coming back down from the top cushion.

The fourth is that the contact on the red will be too thick or thin. If the red is struck too thickly, the cue ball might not get back to baulk. For some reason it's more common for the red to be contacted too thinly, with the result that the cue ball returns too fast, strikes the baulk cushion, and returns half way back towards the blue spot.

A tricky shot is when you are trying to hit the side of the pack from the side and top cushions, glancing off the pack so that the cue ball returns towards baulk. Here make sure you hit the pack on the thin side. If you missed altogether it would not be too serious, but a too thick contact, leaving the cue ball half way up the table and the reds split, could be disastrous.

When fencing for position early in the game, bear all these factors in mind. Know the pitfalls and don't make a mistake yourself. At the same time actively try to put your opponent in a position where he might make a mistake. If you play the early shots as if waiting for something to happen, the chances are it will happen to you – and it will not be to your liking.

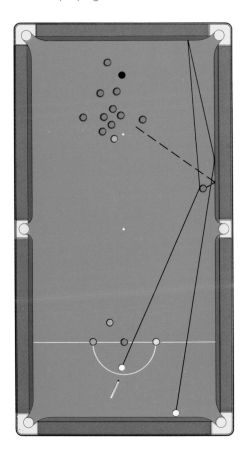

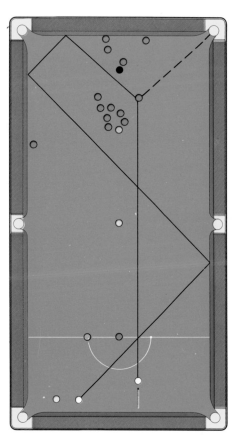

Far left: A path to baulk in which it is necessary to play with right-hand side to bring the cue ball back down the side cushion. Playing without side risks the cue ball hitting a red on its way back from the top cushion.

Left: A path to baulk which combines safety with the possibility of potting a red and finishing on a baulk colour. This is the shot to nothing (see next section).

SHOT TO NOTHING

' The shot to nothing is not always obvious. Even the television commentators, who are experts, are sometimes surprised at a pot that seems to have been plucked out of the air. Always watch out for them – each shot is slightly different from the last and what wasn't on last time might well be this time. '

In snooker, the shot to nothing is like having your cake and eating it.

It usually arises during a period of safety play when the cue ball is being taken to baulk, but can occur at any stage of the game. It means that a player can have a shot at a pot without much risk of leaving anything on for his opponent should he miss. It's a safety shot and a pot attempt.

You should always be on the lookout for the shot to nothing, because the initial pot could easily be the frame-winning shot. Frequently it is in the professional game, where players can capitalize on an opportunity, and know how to retain the initiative they've gained. Nothing is more galling than to see your opponent pot a red without risk, and get a good position on a baulk colour, when you yourself could have played the shot on your turn if only you'd spotted it.

One of the opportunities for a shot to nothing which can be missed is when only one or two reds are in the open, but not pottable, and the others appear to be in a cluster blocking each other's paths to the pockets. Close inspection reveals, however, that a red at the side of the cluster will actually go behind the cluster and pot into the far corner pocket. Don't be afraid to walk up the table to study the reds: because your opponent missed the pot doesn't mean it isn't there.

Another situation to keep an eye on is the plant from among the cluster. Quite often, when the reds have been moved around a bit, two, or perhaps even three, will make a plant into the pocket. As said in the section on plants, these shots are not difficult.

The double to nothing

An opportunity for a shot to nothing which is not often spotted is the double. It's more likely to occur when most of the reds have been potted than earlier in the game. Imagine the last red level with the pink, but apparently safe 2 inches (5cm) from the

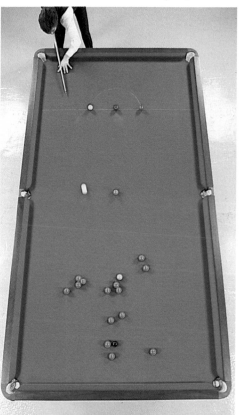

I have spotted that one red in the cluster of three round the pink will go into the top pocket while affording a safe path to baulk (to attempt the red furthest to the left as we look would risk the cue ball going into the other reds, so it would not be a shot to nothing). As you can see I played it too well – I potted the red but unluckily for me put the cue ball right onto the baulk cushion.

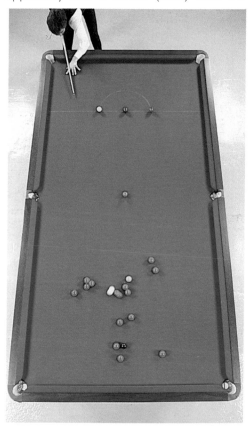

right-hand cushion. The cue ball is in baulk to the left of the green.

If you attempt to double the red into the opposite top pocket, the cue ball will hit the top cushion not too far from the top right-hand pocket. A little check side will ensure that it returns to baulk passing close to the yellow, while, if the shot is played at the right speed, the red, if missed, will stay at the top of the table.

The shot to nothing is a matchwinner if there happens to be a baulk colour, or perhaps a displaced blue, handily over a pocket at the baulk end of the table. If you achieve both your objectives, and pot the red while bringing the cue ball back to safety, you will be rewarded with an easy pot and the opportunity to go back up the table for another red and a big break. This happens often in the professional game.

Of course, you must not lose sight of the fact that the primary object of the shot is safety, so you must check before you attempt any of these pots that the cue ball will take a path back to baulk. There is no point in attempting a pot, narrowly missing it, and then watching the cue ball collide with a red and stay at the top of the table. This, clearly, is not a shot to nothing, but a shot to quite a lot, all of it given away.

Playing positively

There is a psychological danger to the player on a shot to nothing. The tendency is to regard it as 'easy come, easy go' – if you miss the pot you won't leave anything, so you can afford to be a little cavalier in your approach. This is quite wrong, and not only beause you should be concentrating and taking care on every shot. On this particular one you should be taking even more care than usual, if possible. For it can be a matchwinner, and demoralize your opponent. You might think the chance of a shot to nothing is a gift, but there's no need to give it away again. A red potted when you are playing for safety looks to your opponent to be half way to a fluke and can be devastating.

THORBURN'S TIP

● *Don't forget where the object ball is likely to go if the shot to nothing is missed. It is pointless bringing the cue ball back to baulk, for instance, if the red was played as such speed that it came down to baulk with the cue ball, and finished over a pocket.*

' Even the attacking players among the professionals play the shot to nothing which leaves the cue ball on the baulk cushion. When the pot is successful, they roll up to a baulk colour. Although I'm known for safety play, I do not like to play this shot, because if the pot is successful, I prefer the chance to pot a colour. The cue ball tight against the cushion doesn't help me at all. '

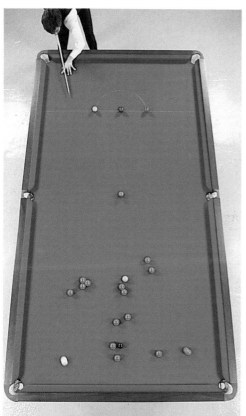

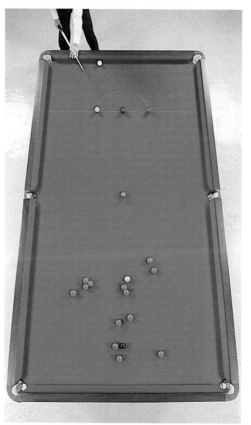

' If you need only the last red to leave your opponent needing snookers, and the red is on a side cushion, and difficult to roll up close behind, play the previous shot to leave the cue ball where you can attempt to double the red into the centre pocket. By playing the double you can bring the cue ball to the end cushion, so that even if you miss you will not leave your opponent on. If instead you had played to pot the red down the cushion, then a miss could leave it over the pocket. In effect, the double is a kind of shot to nothing. '

SAFETY PLAY

So far we have looked at safety play mainly from the point of view of bringing the cue ball back into baulk. But this isn't always possible, and other tactics must be employed.

Even with all the reds still on the table, it pays sometimes to consider the position which would arise if you left the cue ball on the top cushion. It sounds very risky if the reds are partially split to attempt this shot, since any rebound off the top cushion will almost certainly present your opponent with an opportunity for a pot, yet in certain circumstances this shot can be played with great accuracy.

Imagine a loose red 2 or 3 inches (5-8cm) from the top cushion, but at too fine a cut to attempt the pot into the corner pocket from where the cue ball is, in baulk. You're snookered on the cluster by baulk colours and the blue, and other loose reds make the path back to baulk difficult.

It's quite feasible, by playing with drag (see page 45), to hit the red so that it comes away from the cushion while the cue ball stays very close to the cushion. Of course, you must check first that the intended position of the cue ball doesn't present any long pots to the baulk corners or plants into the centre for your opponent. This shot doesn't put your opponent in trouble, because he can usually play a thin shot to return the cue ball to baulk, but at least you might find that the new position is better than the old one.

A similar shot is sometimes used when negotiating a snooker when a number of reds are on the table. Perhaps you've been left behind a baulk colour, and must play off a cushion. Salvation might come from a red, or better a line of two or three, on the top cushion. Playing up slowly to nestle on the top cushion with these reds is usually a safe enough proposition.

Right: One choice here is to trickle into the pack. Even if it means using a little side, make sure you nestle into the pack close to the pink. If you hit the pack too high and too hard you could leave a red on. My choice would probably be that shown by the yellow line. With strong running side I could bring the cue ball off the side and top cushions into the side of the cluster and back down to baulk.

Far right: An example where playing red down towards baulk while leaving the cue ball tight on the top cushion could bring better results than playing the cue ball back to baulk.

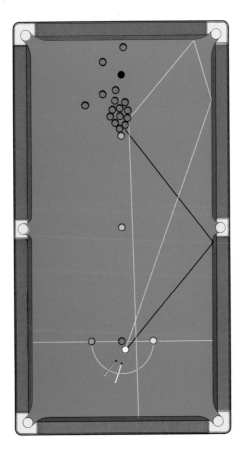

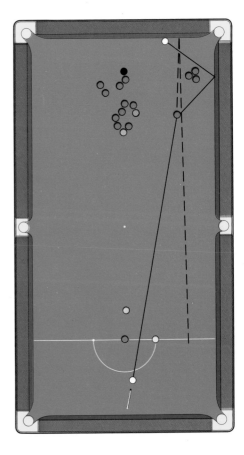

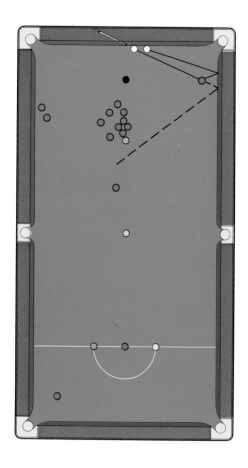

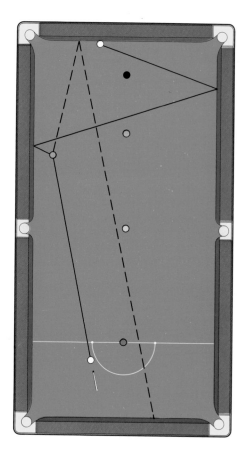

Far left: With a loose red in baulk, you should return to the top cushion using the pack to block the path to the loose red.

Left: An example of doubling the cue ball off two side cushions to the top cushion, while bringing the object ball to the opposite end cushion, in this case for a snooker.

Playing into the pack

Trickling up into the pack is a safety play I'm not fond of, but on occasion it may be the only realistic possibility open to you. The drawback is that you have to play dead-weight, as you do not want to disturb a red and leave it on, and you stand a good chance of leaving a touching ball. This allows your opponent to play the cue ball almost anywhere he chooses to put you in deeper trouble.

Sometimes reds get down into the baulk area, and the top cushion becomes the safety area. What occasionally happens then is that one by one the reds get sent down the table while the cue ball is returned to the top cushion. Don't play these shots automatically. Always search for the shot to nothing down the table, or the shot which your opponent might not expect. For instance, if there are two or three reds in baulk below the green, and the baulk colours are on their spots, it's possible that the line of baulk colours will block a pot of any of them if the cue ball were against the side cushion in the right place. Getting the cue ball there might be easier than bringing it back to the top cushion, and could pay better dividends.

Safety on the black

When the game is on the black, a whole range of safety shots come into their own. Sometimes the angles don't allow the favourite shot of playing the black off the centre of the top cushion to the centre of the bottom cushion, while leaving the cue ball in its place. It's frequently a better bet to try to leave one or both balls tight on the side cushions.

If the black is close to the side cushion on the baulk line, and the cue ball at the other end of the table, it's possible to 'double' the black off the cushion into the centre of the bottom cushion, bringing the cue ball back up to the top of the table. Sometimes you can double the black off two side cushions to the centre of the bottom cushion, while bringing the cue ball back to the top end of the table. Or, you can double the cue ball instead of the black to the bottom cushion, bringing the black to the top end.

All these shots are seen more clearly when only the black is on the table, but of course the principles apply no matter which colour is on. In certain circumstances, and in its own special way, safety play can be as exciting as potting.

POTTING v SAFETY

It's dangerous for a player to think of himself as a 'safety' player or a 'potter': it encourages the neglect of the other aspect of his game, and both are equally important. A potter is likely to develop a 'have a bash at anything' style (you probably know one or two), while the safety player is so busy trying to put his opponent into trouble that he forgets that it's impossible to win on penalties alone and that a few balls must be potted (this type is common enough, too). The best players mix safety and potting according to the state of the game.

The question 'do I attempt the pot or put my opponent in trouble?' occurs frequently in a game, the most obvious example coming after a successful shot to nothing attempt, when the cue ball returns to baulk. Do you roll up behind a colour or try to pot it?

Imagine there is a cluster of six reds left, with one at the back loose, so that if you can

Having potted a red, you have finished just below the brown. The baulk colours are all difficult pots, with no easy way to get up the table for the inviting reds; so you must trickle up behind the brown.

get up there you might begin a break. The colours are on their spots. You must weigh up the chances. If the cue ball is on the cushion, you have little chance of potting a colour. So roll up behind one and leave your opponent an awkward shot.

On the other hand, if you have a three-quarter ball pot of the brown into a centre pocket which will give you an angle to take the cue ball up for the loose red, I would play the pot. If you have an angle on the brown which makes it an easy pot, but leaves the cue ball below the blue, I would still take the pot. Although you can't get at the loose red, you can still play an easy safety shot and put your opponent on the baulk cushion. This is just as uncomfortable a position for him as behind a baulk colour, where he could trickle up to the cluster off a cushion.

The state of the match

Should the actual score of the frame be taken into account? Sometimes it must, but in my view not as much as many players think. For example, some players will say that if you are 40 or 50 behind, and there isn't much more on the table, you must go for everything. Conversely if you are that much ahead, you must take no risks.

My opinion is that if a shot is a good percentage shot, with a better chance of scoring a few points than giving a few away, then it's a good percentage shot irrespective of the score. I would moderate this view in the following situation. If I needed all the balls on the table, and they were all in open positions, and a difficult potting chance arose, I might well take it. My reasoning would be that one good shot could win the match. It's make or break time. If I wait for a better chance, two or three of the balls might in the meantime get knocked to safe positions. I would then need to get in two or three times, and the one good shot is probably the better percentage chance.

If I was the player ahead, however, I would decline a difficult pot if a miss could let my opponent in. I would play safe and seek a chance of putting a ball or two safe so that he couldn't win in one visit to the table.

While we're discussing the state of the score, let me make this point. Suppose there

THORBURN'S TIPS

● *Safety play doesn't look as spectacular as potting, but for connoisseurs it's just as enthralling, and in my opinion it wins more matches at the top level of the game.*

● *Don't get mesmerized in a safety duel. It is possible for you to concentrate so hard on getting the ball safe for shot after shot that you overlook a potting chance when it arises.*

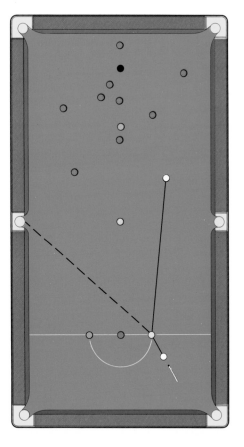

are four reds left on the table – a possible 59 points if all are taken with blacks. Your opponent is 50 ahead. There's no need for panic measures. You can win even if the black is tight on a cushion, and you don't need it with any of the reds. You can win with one break, or maybe two or three. And don't forget this – it's unlikely that your opponent can win without potting another ball, so he has to make a break, too. There's no reason to risk all on a dubious shot. Don't think it's 'make or break' time when it's just beginning to get a bit sticky.

Left: The balls are in the same positions as in the illustration opposite, but this time the cue ball has finished where you can pot the yellow into the middle pocket. The natural angle will take the cue ball up the table for a red, and this time you should choose the pot.

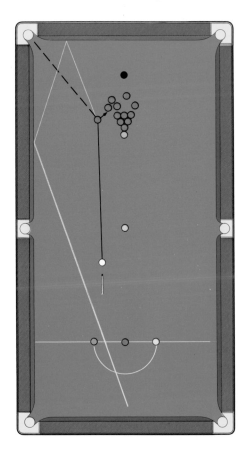

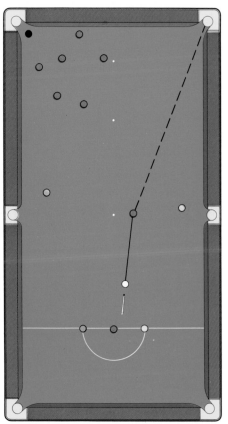

Far left: You can pot the loose red. But this is not a shot to nothing, as the cue ball will go into the pack, and you could even end snookered on all the colours. The pot is too risky. Better to play the red into the pack, splitting the other reds and bringing the cue ball back to baulk as shown by the yellow line.

Left: The black is guarding the top left-hand pocket. The best shot is to attempt to pot the red as shown, stunning the cue ball to get on pink or blue, rather than the black, which when respotted will go into only one top pocket.

SNOOKERS

You could describe the snooker as the best form of safety shot, but it's more than that. It should be an aggressive attacking stroke. Too often I see snookers laid almost mechanically, as if it is the right thing to do. Sometimes a pot is declined because a snooker opportunity presents itself, but frequently the snooker is so easy to get out of that it was hardly worth the trouble to lay.

Think of the snooker as a constructive shot, and work out what you're intending to do with it. The value of the snooker is not the penalty points it brings, except in those end-game situations where a player needs to inflict a penalty to win, i.e. he's 30 points behind with only the colours on the table.

An example of what I mean is often seen when a player trickles up behind a baulk colour to snooker his opponent on a number of reds. Many players, anxious not to fall short of the object ball, play the shot too hard, to leave 2 inches (5cm) between the balls, and then retire satisfied with the snooker. But it's a simple task for the opponent to roll up to the cluster of reds off one cushion.

In this situation you should not only be trying to get tight on the baulk colour, but also assessing the most difficult angle for your opponent to play up the table. By playing the cue ball to one side or other of the baulk colour you can force him to play off one or other side cushion, making his task more tricky. You can perhaps force him to play off the back and side cushion.

No two situations at the table are ever quite the same, and you could fill a whole book with diagrams of how to set snookers. It would be more useful, I think, if I tried to isolate a few principles governing what makes a good one.

Splitting the reds

If you're laying a good snooker early in the

Right: An example of the area which can be blocked off by two balls on their spots – in this case green and blue. This helps show the importance of the opening break. Even with the ball on the cushion, much of this area is covered.

Far right: If you have an easy opportunity for a snooker, such as here behind the green and brown, it will pay you dividends to use the object ball to split the pack, making it very difficult for your opponent to play safe.

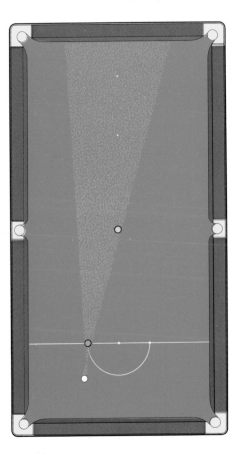

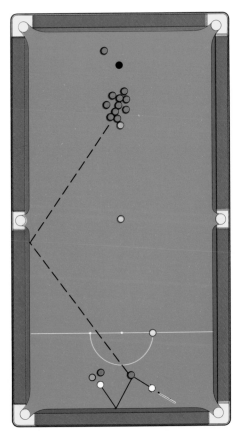

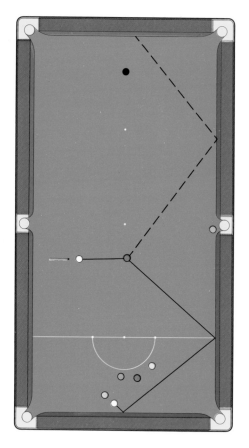

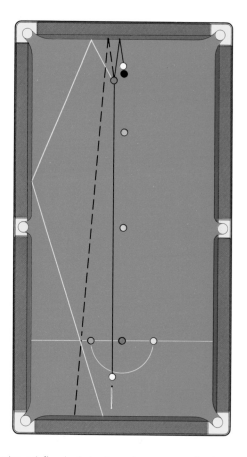

Far left: In laying a
snooker on the last
red as illustrated,
where it is possible to
play either the red or
the cue ball to baulk,
it is better to put the
cue ball behind the
colours.

Left: You have two
choices. First, a stun
shot leaving the cue
ball behind the black
and the red at the
baulk end. If you are
leading, however, it
might be better to
knock the red onto the
black, knocking the
black safe, and
returning the cue ball
to baulk as shown by
the yellow line.

game, it's to your advantage to open the
balls up. You have the initiative, and the first
opportunity of a pot is likely to fall to you, so
you give yourself the maximum chance of an
easy red.

For example, let's assume that most of the
reds are still in a cluster, except one, which is
in baulk, just below and to the right of
yellow. The cue ball is just below the red,
with an angle to make it easy to play slowly
onto the red, pushing it past the yellow, and
rest just behind the yellow. It is a snooker,
but it would not be difficult for your
opponent to trickle up to the cluster, leaving
you a shot with awkward cueing and the
one loose red down near the yellow.

A much better shot (although more
difficult) is to play the red hard up the table
into the cluster, while leaving the cue ball
behind the yellow as before by means of a
stun shot. Now, with the reds split, and
probably two or three on, your opponent
will be faced with a difficult shot to get the
cue ball safe.

The opportunity to split the reds occurs
more usually when you are playing from
near the cluster down the table to tuck the
cue ball behind a colour or two near the
baulk cushion. If the red you come off can be

played firmly into the cluster to split them,
your opponent has much more difficulty in
getting the cue ball safe.

What you must avoid, obviously, is
leaving a red over a pocket, and failing to lay
the snooker.

Areas for snookers

When watching the professionals, you
might be impressed by the accuracy with
which they can lay a snooker behind a
colour while sending the cue ball the length
of the table, perhaps off a cushion.
Sometimes this is an illusion, and if you look
at the angles you might discover that the
player had a large area into which to aim.
There was actually quite a big margin for
error.

Put the blue and brown on their spots,
and the cue ball on the semi-circle of the 'D'
just to the left of the brown, so that it
couldn't quite be played up the table
between the blue and brown. Now stoop
and, with your eye just above the baulk
cushion, see how much of the top of the
table you can't play the cue ball into without
hitting a cushion. The blue and brown block
out most of the right-hand side. If the cue
ball were in fact the object ball, you would

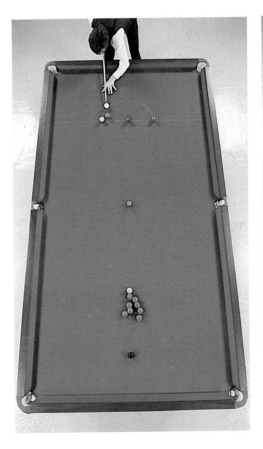 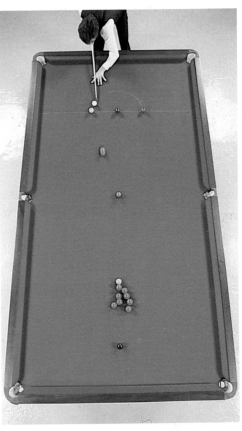

have all that area in which to leave the cue ball to lay a snooker.

Let's put this into practice. Suppose the last red is not pottable, near the left-hand side cushion, just above the pink, while the cue ball is between black and pink, so that you can double the red across the table to a position above and to the right of the pink, i.e. into the area you've just been looking at. The cue ball naturally runs towards baulk, and you try to get it on the cushion, say, more or less below the green. If you succeed with the cue ball, the red will almost look after itself. There's an area about 18 inches (45cm) wide in which it can stop to provide the snooker. If your opponent can get through a narrow gap between blue and brown to hit the red you're unlucky. It's far more likely to be a good snooker, one which might leave you on the red next shot.

Be aware of the use you can make of the brown, blue, pink and black being in line. A cue ball just below the brown or above the black will have a wide area of the table blocked off by this line of balls.

Using the cue ball
When laying a snooker, either the cue ball or the object ball must be placed behind one of the other balls. But it's better if you can make this the cue ball, and for three reasons.

First, the cue ball is easier to control than the object ball. You're much more likely to be able to place it precisely.

Second, the nearer the cue ball is to the snookering ball, the more of the table is blocked out. For example, if the cue ball is not quite below the yellow, and the object ball is up the table, it's likely that the cue ball can't be played anywhere near the object ball except off a cushion. On the other hand, if it were the object ball not quite behind the yellow, it could possibly be hit directly.

Third, the more the object ball is out in the open, preferably near the centre of the table, the more chance there is of your opponent missing it. The snooker which tucks the object ball up behind another ball near the cushion can usually be negotiated quite easily off that cushion.

A good general rule in snookering is to get as much space between the cue ball and object ball as possible. Any slight mis-calculation of the angle off the cushion could mean your opponent will miss.

A frequent snooker opportunity occurs when the last red, say, is next to the black, which is on its spot. The cue ball is near the

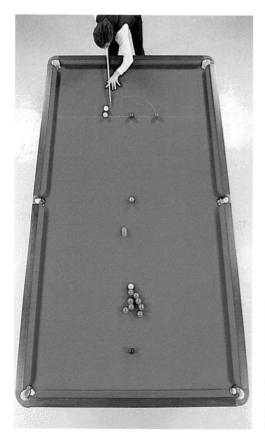

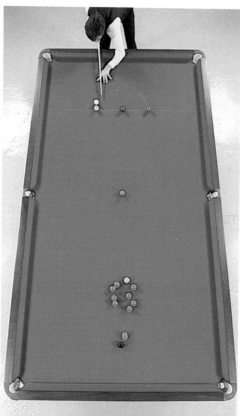

I am following one of the ideas mentioned in the text. In stunning behind the yellow and playing the loose red hard into the pack, I have split the reds invitingly but left my opponent snookered on them all with a difficult escape to attempt.

blue spot. It's a poor option to play up to the red slowly, hoping to push it just beyond the black while the cue ball stops just short of the black. Much better to play the shot firmly, so the red travels back off the cushion down the table, while stunning the cue ball off the cushion to rest behind the black. It's a safer shot for you and a more difficult snooker.

Snookering is a question of being familiar with angles, which is what snooker is largely about. Use snookers positively, with a definite purpose in view, rather than as a sort of holding shot to cramp your opponent.

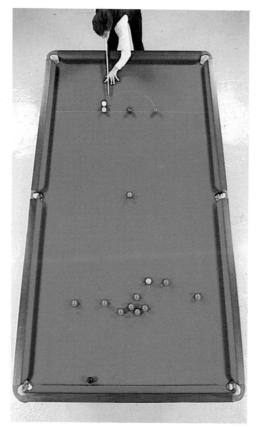

THORBURN'S TIPS

● *Bear in mind what you might leave if you fail to lay the intended snooker. If the snooker will leave an object ball in a pottable position near a pocket, it might be better just to knock it safe than risk the snooker going wrong.*
● *The best snookers leave the object ball in the open and the cue ball a long way from it. This gives your opponent the maximum chance of missing the object ball and leaving it on for you.*

NEGOTIATING SNOOKERS

❝ It is possible to distort the angle a ball leaves a cushion without side. I won money gambling on the following shot. With reds on each end of the baulk line and another in the centre of the bottom cushion, I would bet I could play the cue ball from the side cushion level with the pink spot to hit one side cushion, the bottom cushion and the other side cushion, all in baulk, and return up the table without hitting a red. The shot cannot be performed with side. The secret is to play it with strong backspin. The backspin distorts the angle at which the cue ball leaves the cushion. Many players would try to copy this shot without being able to do it. Try this shot and note the angle at which the cue ball comes off the cushion because you'll find that this is a good shot for getting out of snookers. ❞

Right: It is better to play this shot off two cushions, as shown, to leave the cue ball on the pocket side of the red, than off one cushion, which could leave an easy pot.

Far right: This snooker is easier to negotiate off two cushions, as shown, than off the baulk cushion only.

Negotiating snookers requires the same skill as setting them – a good knowledge of angles. One difference is that while snookers might be laid accidentally, rarely do you escape from one by accident.

One way of getting out of a snooker is to use swerve, but although this might seem the most direct method, it's used mostly as a last resort. An exception is when a player near the end of the game is defending a lead against an opponent who needs a snooker or two. His only objective is to avoid giving away a penalty, and a gentle swerve is sometimes the surest way of hitting the object ball. If he should leave it on it doesn't matter – in fact as he wants the balls to disappear it could even be to his advantage. In ordinary situations in the middle of a match, however, the careful use of the cushions is normally a better way of keeping control of the shot than using swerve.

Most escape shots are played at a slow pace. You're on the defensive if you are snookered, and it's not a time to send the balls careering around the table; this can help only your opponent. Just as I advised splitting the reds when setting a snooker, I suggest you shouldn't disturb them when getting out of one. Playing gently into the pack doesn't necessarily put your opponent in trouble, but sometimes it's the only way to play for time – and perhaps your next shot will give you a better opportunity to play aggressively.

The pace of the shot is just as important if you're playing at a single red. A situation which often arises is when the red is on the top cushion, 2 or 3 inches (5-8cm) from the right-hand pocket. You have to play it, and are snookered behind the brown or yellow. You play to come off the right-hand cushion. You don't want to play firmly, because the balls might go anywhere, so you nestle against the red, pocket side.

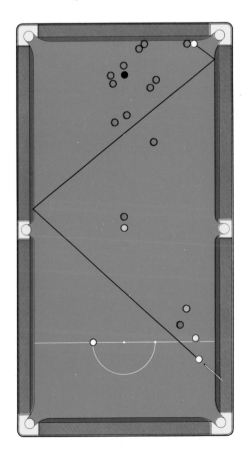

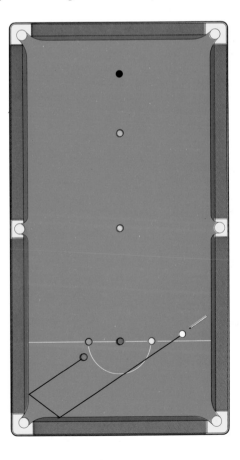

Those last two words pinpoint another requirement to bear in mind. If possible, keep the cue ball on the pocket side of the object ball. This avoids the possibility of negotiating the snooker only to leave a simple pot.

Sometimes this principle will involve playing off two cushions, when you could have made contact off one. Suppose, on the previous shot, you couldn't contact the red off the right-hand cushion because there were balls in the way. You must go off the left-hand cushion. You could go off the left-hand cushion only, but this time you will finish on the other side of the object ball, with the possibility of leaving a pot into the corner. Better to go off the left-hand cushion at such an angle as to hit the right-hand cushion near the top pocket, and to come off onto the red from that direction. Judge the shot to land on the red on the pocket side — and be careful not to go across the red.

To aim for the safe side of the red, as in this example, is almost like erring on the side of safety. If you miss, the referee might call it an intentional miss. You must never make a deliberate miss, of course; always try to hit the ball, even if you're trying to hit it on one side. If the referee calls a miss, accept it as the rub of the green. It's more important that your conscience is clear.

Coming off two cushions can actually be the easier way to hit the object ball in some cases. Suppose the black is on its spot, and another ball is practically touching it just below it. The cue ball is to the right of this barrier of two balls, and the object ball near the side cushion, hidden by them. You can play to hit the object ball off the top cushion, but it's even safer to hit it off the top and side cushions. The proximity of the cushion widens the target.

Occasions arise where there's not much you can do to ensure leaving the balls safe, e.g. when the object ball is in the centre of the table. It's almost a case of hit and hope. This is why in the section on snookering I advised leaving the object ball in the open.

THORBURN'S TIP

● *The danger in trying to negotiate a snooker lies less in the four points you will concede if you miss, than in the position you could leave your opponent. So consider where the balls will go when deciding how you will attempt to hit the object ball.*

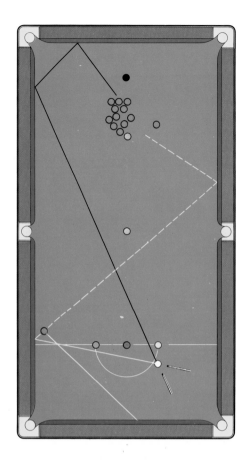

This is a useful angle to know. From behind the yellow you can play the cue ball to nestle up to the pack from the top cushion. My preference would be the shot shown by the yellow line, hitting the red behind the green off the cushion, bringing the cue ball back to the bottom cushion and sending the red up the table.

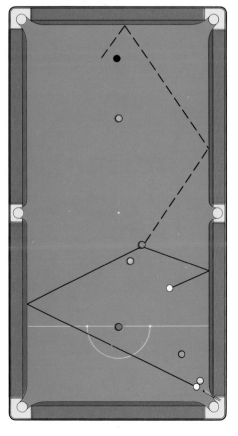

An example of a good snooker. There is little one can do but hit and hope. You could try to pot the red into the middle pocket, which would be a bonus, but try to get the cue ball and object ball in different halves of the table. The result illustrated is perfect.

POSITIONAL PLAY

❛ When I first started to play, somebody told me that Joe Davis claimed to think nine or ten shots ahead on every shot. Then it occurred to me that if Joe had a bad night and spoiled his position on his first shot, he then had immediately to think up a new set of ten shots. I soon discovered that there was no truth in the story and this made me feel a lot better. ❜

How many shots ahead should you plan? Not more than three or four at the most, I would say. What I do have in mind, however, when the opportunity for a break occurs, is a general awareness of how the balls lie. I make a mental note of any problem balls for potting, together with any that are blocking the path to the pocket of other balls. I don't say to myself: 'I'll pot this red, stun for the black, take that red, run-through for the black into this pocket, come off the cushion to there' – and so on – but I do know the general direction of the break and will be re-assessing the situation every time I pot a ball. Chalking the tip of my cue affords thinking time.

It is, of course, necessary with every shot to know what you're going to do with the cue ball; and in order to decide what to do with it, you must have the next shot in mind. That probably extends to the shot after that, too, because you'll want to know what

angle to get on to the second shot. But beyond that planning can get rather speculative.

The art of positional play is based on knowing how the cue ball behaves after any particular shot. If you've followed carefully the advice given in this book so far you'll now have a good idea of how to control the cue ball. In the old days, billiards players were reckoned to be able to tackle snooker players at their own game much more successfully than the other way round, because all billiards players knew how to control the cue ball. These days, with snooker having outstripped billiards in popularity in most parts of the world, the difference hardly exists, but you might notice that the good billiards players, like Rex Williams, are also very good on cue ball control in snooker.

One aspect of positional play is the negative one of keeping out of trouble. The simplest way to find unwanted difficulties is to leave the cue ball tight on a cushion after a pot, making the next one that much more difficult. It's easily done and sometimes happens to the best players, even when they've foreseen the danger.

A more disastrous happening is the in-off, and this possibility is easily overlooked. Some shots attract the in-off, and I've found them by experience. One is the plain half-ball pot into a top pocket, with the cue ball having to travel almost straight up the table to contact the object ball. The pot is made, the cue ball hits the centre of the top cushion, the side cushion about level with the pink, and runs straight into a baulk pocket. How often do you see this in the big tournaments?

Perhaps the pot was a shot to nothing, but the in-off can still be costly. If you're aware of its possibility you might avoid the accident. Equally annoying is being left a red 2 or 3 inches (5-8cm) from the top pocket. You play from around the 'D', cut it in, only to find the cue ball coming off the top cushion almost diagonally across the table into the baulk pocket.

Centre pockets are frequently traps for the in-off. From near the side cushion, just below the black spot, you play across the

There is an easy red into the top right-hand corner, but it is better to take this opportunity to pot the red shown, staying on the black and developing the other three reds. The easy red is still there for next time.

table parallel to the top cushion for a half-ball pot of a red into the top pocket, the cue ball hits the far cushion and doubles back into the centre pocket beside you. Or, from the top cushion near a pocket, you cut a black from its spot into the opposite top pocket. The cue ball has a nasty habit of running on into the centre pocket.

Potting into the centre pockets from certain angles can lead the cue ball to a corner pocket, too. If you're below the blue, which is on its spot, with about a three-quarter pot into the centre pocket, the cue ball could easily go straight into the top pocket, unless you guard against it. Or, with a ball 6 inches (15cm) or so from a centre pocket, and the cue ball around the 'D', you cut the object ball nicely into the centre pocket only to see the cue ball proceed up the table into the top pocket.

There are in-off traps all round the table for the unwary — and those mentioned here seem to occur rather more often than they should. But perhaps they are still rare enough for you not to notice that you often go in-off from a certain situation. All you can do is watch out for these traps, and their relations. They can all be avoided, of course, by various degrees of screw or side.

Gaining position

A more positive aspect of positional play is gaining position for the next pot.

Suppose a red is 6 inches (15cm) from a centre pocket and just above it: it's a simple pot because the cue ball is half way between the blue and pink spots. The natural angle of the pot takes the cue ball into the side cushion above the centre pocket at right angles, and a soft shot leaves the blue on into the opposite centre pocket. If you overlook the fact that after the blue you need to be up the table for the next red, you will pot the first red as described and be on the 'wrong side' of the blue. An awareness of positional play would tell you instinctively that you must play the red with running side to get on the baulk side of the blue for position on the second red.

Sometimes you must play with side not so much to take the cue ball into the exact position, but to prevent hitting another ball and spoiling your position. For example, you have a half-ball pot of a red into the corner, but you realize that the natural angle will bring the cue ball back off the top cushion to cannon into the black, your intended next ball. You avoid this by playing check side or running side, according to which side of the

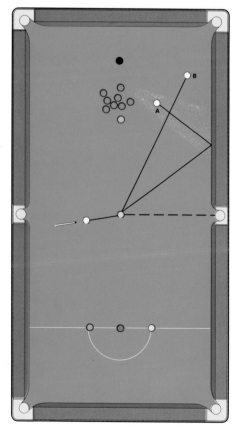

Potting the red as shown will free the others for the top right-hand pocket. It is a better option than potting the other straight red and trying to get position off the black for the three in a cluster. You might not get as good an opportunity to split these reds.

❝ If you are on the baulk side of the blue, with a half-ball pot into the centre pocket, it is easy to go in-off into the top pocket, and I still do it myself a couple of times a year. A little side will allow you to make the pot while running the cue ball to the top cushion rather than into the pocket. Get to know these angles from the blue when using side. You will be able to use this knowledge sometimes to help you cannon into a red and set up a pot to continue the break. ❞

To pot the blue and get position on the loose red at the top of the pack, the cue ball should finish somewhere in the shaded area. Shot A, using the cushion, is safer than shot B, where the cue ball runs across the desired area.

black you would prefer the cue ball to be.

On the whole, it's best if you can obtain the position you want without side or spin of any kind. With plain ball shots the cue ball is going in its natural direction, and its control should be easier.

The direction of the shot

You'll find positional play easiest if you can manage to get the cue ball running in the direction of the next pot rather than away from it, since it then gives you more margin for error. It helps if the ball is running along the line of the next shot rather than across it. For example, imagine you're potting the green from above the yellow spot. You want to get onto the right of the cluster of reds, as one of them pots into the top left-hand pocket. Inexperienced players might play the cue ball to come off the side cushion above the green across to the right of the reds – but I would play the shot to come off the cushion at a narrower angle, so that it crosses the table and comes off the other side cushion just above the centre pocket to run towards the reds. The reason is that the ball is travelling roughly on the line of the next pot. If I misjudge the speed a little, I'll be further from, or nearer to, the red than I

anticipated, but the pot is still on. With the other shot, the ball cuts across the line of the next shot more or less at right angles. Too much or too little pace will alter the angle for the pot, and might even mean it's not on.

Any balls which block pockets for other balls are a nuisance. I take the first opportunities which occur to pot these, or nudge them aside. It makes succeeding positional play easier if all the pockets are available.

One of the most satisfying aspects of positional play is the moving of an awkward ball off a cushion while potting another ball. For example, there's an awkward red near the left-hand cushion, just below the pink spot. You're below the blue, which is on its spot, with a half-ball pot into the centre pocket. The natural angle takes the cue ball to the top cushion and back down to come off the side cushion just above the red to nudge it into the open.

The shot has a margin for error, because you could use side if not quite in the right position on the blue. It's best to play a shot like this when another red is pottable, so there's one 'in reserve' if the nudge on the awkward red doesn't develop it. This is all part of the skill of positional play.

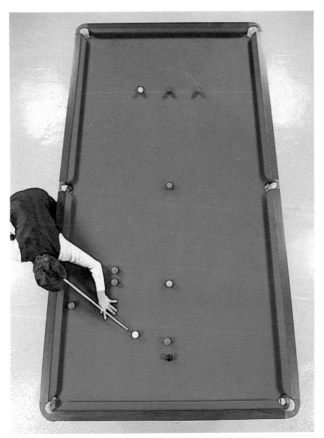

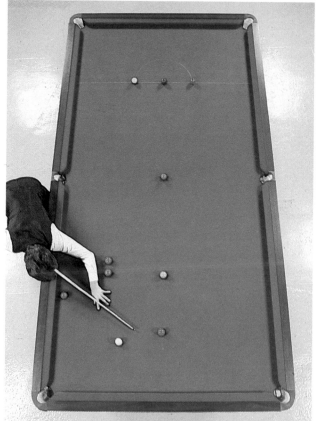

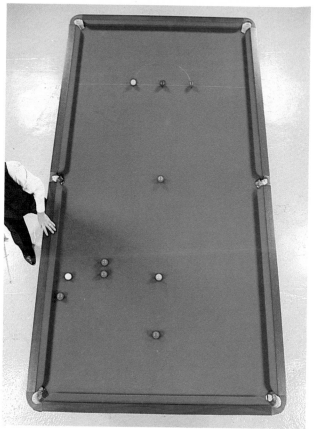

USING THE BLUE

Most century breaks are made with a succession of reds and blacks. But occasionally the blue can be very useful in keeping a break going if things go temporarily wrong around the black spot. It's better potting a red with a good firm shot to get position on the blue than trying a more delicate shot in order to get on the pink or black, which you might not stroke properly.

Frequently you'll find yourself nicely among the reds, but the black and pink are tied up. Sometimes a red gets so close to the black that you cannot pot it, while the pink is often mixed up with the reds. So you're forced to use the blue to build a break.

The prime object is to bring the cue ball down to just *below* the blue. If you can get a three-quarter ball pot, then you can bring the cue ball back up the table for the next red, and, by the use of spin, have a range of options as to which red to get on and how.

Sometimes you can stun or screw back to get good position when going for the blue, but more often you'll be running down off the top cushion or the top and side cushions, and in trying not to go too far past the blue you fall a little short. If you finish dead level on the blue you're probably committed to a longish red for your next shot, but if you're above the blue you can get back off one or more cushions.

From the wrong side of the blue, the half-ball pot is probably the least troublesome, although none of these shots is easy, because the cue ball is going into baulk and you must avoid hitting any of the baulk colours on the way down or back.

From a position on the left side of the table, you can stun down between brown and yellow, and check side (which will be right-hand side) will bring the cue ball back between the same colours. Aim to keep the cue ball nearer the yellow on the way down, or you might clip the brown on the way back. The cue ball will come fairly centrally up the table, just to the left of the pink spot.

Using two cushions

An alternative shot from the same position would be to play it with running (left-hand) side. The cue ball takes the same path to the baulk cushion, but the running side then throws it to the right-hand side cushion, and returns it back up the table round the yellow.

This makes it more certain that the cue ball will miss the baulk colours on its return. It follows a path which will take it to the left-hand side of the table, so if there are two or three reds which will go into the top right-hand pocket you should land on one of them at a convenient angle.

If you have a much fuller angle than three-quarter ball on the blue you won't have enough angle to stun down to the baulk

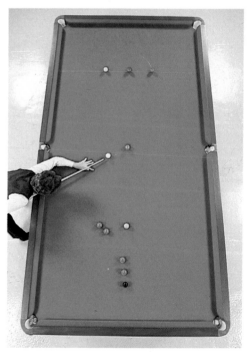

cushion and back up to the reds, so you'll need to use three cushions. Assuming you are again on the left-hand side of the table, pot the blue with some power, applying topspin and right-hand side, striking the cue ball at about 2 o'clock. The cue ball will run through to the right-hand cushion, take a wide angle to about the centre of the baulk cushion, and come back up the table from the left-hand side cushion, thus going all round the baulk colours.

If you get on to the blue so poorly that the

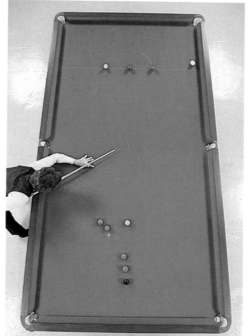

I have played for the blue but finished above it. I would play running side if reasonably near to the blue and check side if further away. On this occasion I played with strong right-hand side, went into baulk between brown and green and came back off the side cushion near the baulk line onto two of the reds.

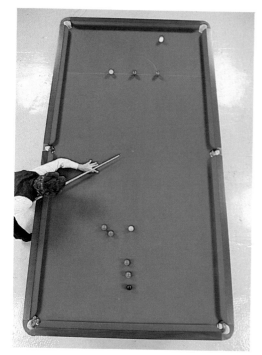

pot into the centre pocket is about quarter-ball, you can still stun down to the baulk cushion and come back up using side, but you'll have to judge your angles carefully to

avoid the baulk colours. If the pot of the blue is a cut, the question arises as to whether it's better to take the pot into the baulk pocket, screwing back for the red.

It's easy to practise these shots. Put the baulk colours and the blue on their spots, and vary the position of the cue ball to give yourself different angles into the middle pocket. Play to get back up the table. With practice you won't have to replace a baulk colour too often.

THORBURN'S TIPS

● While it is possible to make quite a big break by using the blue and/or the baulk colours, always look for the opportunity when potting a red to disturb the balls which are tying up the pink and black so that you can revert to the more normal and easier top-of-the-table play.

● Sometimes a red or two get knocked towards the blue spot, and can be used if position is lost at the top of the table. A short red-blue-red sequence can help regain prime position on the black.

USING THE SMALL COLOURS

‘ If position at the top of the table is lost, the fact that there are three baulk colours in a line at the other end of the table is very useful. Any shot which takes the cue ball near to baulk after a red is almost sure to leave a colour on. ’

In potting a red you'll sometimes misjudge an attempt to get on the blue and finish too far down the table. This should be no problem as the baulk colours offer plenty of opportunities to get back up the table. You can use the small colours in break-building just as well as the blue, and may have to if the blue has been knocked off its spot.

Unlike the situation with the blue, here you want the cue ball to finish *above* the baulk colours because it's easier to pot them into the baulk pockets. You can pot the baulk colours into the middle pockets from their spots, but the angle of the pocket makes the pot more difficult, especially at the pace needed to get the cue ball up the table.

You have a wide variety of angles at your disposal if the cue ball finishes above the baulk line because there will be at least two of the baulk colours to pot, one at a fuller angle than the other.

Suppose you finish directly above the yellow spot, with a straight full-ball pot of the brown into the left-hand baulk pocket. You can pot the brown with deep screw to bring the cue ball straight back to the cushion. The ball will meet the right-hand

side cushion about 10 inches (25cm) below the centre pocket. Played without side the cue ball will leave the cushion and cross the table between the blue and pink spots, about 10 inches (25cm) below the pink. Played with check (right-hand) side, the cue ball will cross nearer to the blue spot, and with running side it will run up towards the black.

If the cue ball finishes near the right-hand cushion with a straight pot of the yellow into the left-hand baulk pocket, a pot played with screw alone would take the cue ball across the table just below the blue spot. With running side you could bring the cue ball up below the pink.

Alternatively, you would have from this

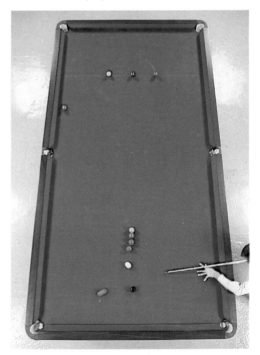

position something like a half-ball pot on the brown. Potting the brown plain ball would take the cue ball to the left-hand side cushion to bring it across the table in the other direction, just below the blue. Running (right-hand) side will take the cue ball above the blue. Without using side, you could pot the brown with stun run-through, so that the cue ball runs through to contact the side cushion just below the centre

● *Don't scorn the baulk colours as aids to keeping a break going. Just as the points given away by a foul are usually less important than the ending of a break or the giving away of position, so the five points 'lost' by taking yellow instead of black are less important than keeping control of your break.*

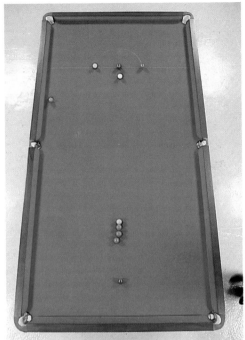

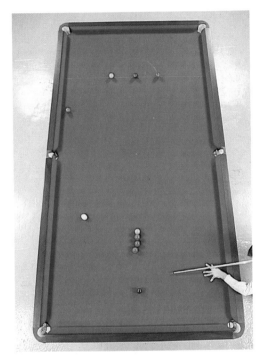

Here I would go down for a baulk colour. It is possible to roll in the red to stay on the black, but there is a risk attached, and as you can see a natural plain-ball pot with no side has taken the cue ball perfectly onto green or yellow to get back for the reds.

and leave them where they finish on the table. Then pot the brown full-ball, using screw and side.

When playing for the baulk colours, beware of ending below the baulk line.

pocket to run up to just below the pink. Or you could use deep screw to take the cue ball almost straight up the table.

Choice of shots

I hope you can see that the possibilities are endless. A three-quarter ball pot on the brown might be a half-ball pot on the yellow or green — you can take your pick. If the cue ball finishes above the baulk line, a little on the yellow side of the brown, you might have a three-quarter ball angle on the yellow and a half-ball angle on the green.

There's no hardship, then, in having to go down the table after potting a red. The baulk colours will almost certainly provide an opportunity to get back to the pack.

Practise by putting the brown on its spot and potting it from a half-ball angle into the baulk pockets, using plain ball contact and then running side. Use the reds as cue balls

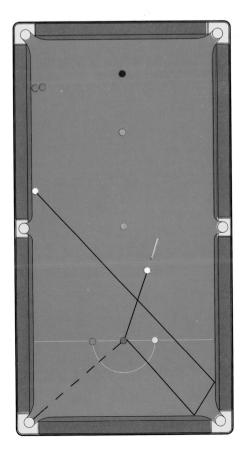

This shot on the brown is one which frequently crops up. The baulk and side cushions are used to bring the cue ball back to position on the reds.

SPLITTING THE REDS

The subject of splitting the pack of reds arose when we discussed snookers, the general point being that it's better from your point of view to split the reds when you're placing your opponent in difficulties, as you are the more likely to benefit. Splitting the reds in order to keep a break going, however, is a different proposition. Usually a break at the beginning of a game starts with two or three loose reds, the rest being in the pack. Sooner or later they must be split.

The most common way of splitting the pack is to get an angle on the black so that the cue ball can hit the centre of the top cushion and come back at something like a right angle to the cushion to split the reds. This isn't guaranteed to split them so that a red is left on. Sometimes, however, you can improve your chances by thinking a shot or two ahead.

If you have two or three reds to pot before you need to split the pack, and one of them is over a pocket, don't leave splitting the pack to the last red. Keeping the easy red as insurance, get an angle on the black to split the pack by clipping it on the side where the easy red lies. If the reds don't split to your advantage, you have the easy red to fall back on, and can have a second chance to split the reds. As they will have been loosened by your previous shot, this second attempt ought to develop one or two into pottable positions.

Sometimes you can earn yourself two shots at the pack by bearing the blue in mind. For example, you have a loose red at the top and slightly to one side of the pack. It would be easy to leave the cue ball so that it's more or less a straight pot, allowing you to run through onto the black and thus gaining position to pot the black and split the reds. You're thinking two shots in advance.

But suppose you were to leave the cue

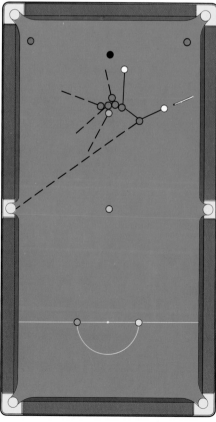

Right: This shot must be played constantly in practice before you play it in a match, but it pays dividends if you can do it. The red into the middle pocket, as shown, will split the pack, with the cue ball ending on the black (or the brown, which is additional insurance). The red to the top corner is still there if the split is unfavourable.

Far right: Instead of getting on the black, you can go down for the blue, splitting the reds on the way.

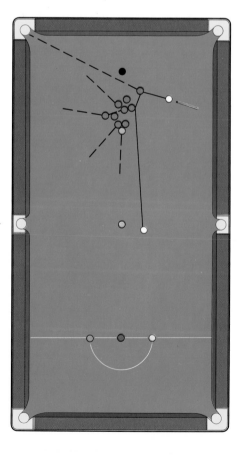

ball 3 inches (8cm) further up the table; instead of running through onto the black, you can pot the red with screw to run the cue ball into the side of the cluster so that it runs down for the blue.

If you're lucky you'll have dislodged a couple of reds so that you can pot the blue and gain position for one of them. If you're unlucky, you can pot the blue and again run into the cluster, which, as it is now loosened, should behave better this time. In any case, you've given yourself two chances. This might be said to be thinking three shots in advance.

Be positive

Some cautious players are reluctant to split the pack before they have potted all the loose reds on the grounds that they don't want to risk leaving a chance for their opponent if the reds split unfavourably. Even more caution is shown by players who clear up any loose reds and then play for safety off the pack. Your attitude should be that you must play the positive shot. It won't always work out for you, and you'll sometimes make mistakes, but it's the only way to improve your game, so be brave.

Similarly, don't be afraid of attempting to split the pack even if it makes the pot slightly more difficult. Always try to keep breaks going because while you're at the table you have the advantage. If you play for safety, the next player to begin a break is as likely to be your opponent.

When the pack still resembles its triangular shape, it is better to split it from above. If the cue ball runs into the side of the pack from the blue spot, it's likely to slide off towards the corner pocket.

Once the pack has been loosened a little, you can work out the likeliest angle to run into it. It will also probably be the angle which provides the widest target.

THORBURN'S TIP

● *It isn't necessary to play the cue ball hard into the pack when splitting them. How often do you see the cue ball slam into the pack and bury itself while reds go everywhere? Often a soft oblique contact will nudge a couple of reds free with the cue ball nicely behind them.*

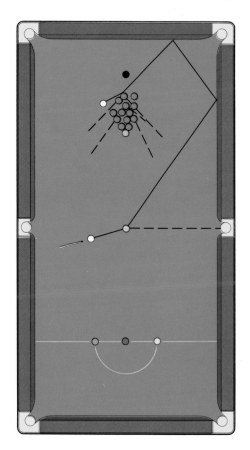

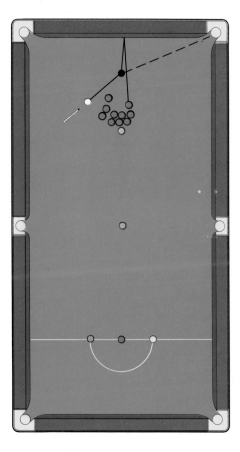

Far left: Running directly into the pack from the blue will probably make the cue ball slide off towards a corner pocket. Splitting the pack from above, as shown, is likely to be more profitable.

Left: With a half-ball angle on the black, it is a good idea to use the pack to stop the cue ball as shown, leaving the loose red into the top pocket. It is easy to get on this red without hitting the pack, but you should use the chance to split the reds.

CONTROLLING THE ANGLES

The most important ball on the table is the cue ball. No matter where the other balls are, it's the position of the cue ball which determines whether or not a break is on. This is lucky, for while you're at the table the cue ball is the ball most under your control. It is, after all, the one you hit. With every shot you have a number of places into which you can place the ball; and to identify these places, you must know what happens to the cue ball after it strikes the object ball.

If the cue ball, struck in the centre, makes half-ball contact with the object ball, it will deviate from its path by an angle of about 45 degrees. The angle varies slightly with the force – the harder you hit the cue ball, the wider the angle. This is the widest angle the cue ball will take with plain-ball striking.

If the cue ball strikes the object ball at full-ball contact, it will follow the path of the object ball. Anything between full-ball and half-ball contact, and the cue ball will deviate by between 0 degrees and 45 degrees, according to the angle. If the cue ball strikes the object ball at less than half-ball (i.e. from half-ball to the finest of cuts) then, while the object ball will be sent at a wider angle, the cue ball will again deviate at an angle of from 45 to nearly 0 degrees.

You can get to know the angles which half-ball pots create by potting the colours off their spots. It's interesting to note that a half-ball pot of the black from its spot sends the cue ball to the top cushion and back down the centre of the table over the black and pink spots. A half-ball pot of the pink into the top pocket takes the cue ball in-off into the middle pocket off the side cushion.

Discover the angles the cue ball takes after a plain-ball pot of the colours from their spots at three-quarter ball angle. Notice that the three-quarter ball pot of the black off its spot, if the cue ball is below the black, sends the cue ball off the top cushion towards the centre pocket on the same side of the table as the pot. On the other hand, if the cue ball is above the black spot, the three-quarter ball pot will take it from the side cushion towards the opposite centre pocket.

You can repeat these exercises with contacts of quarter-ball and less to familiarize yourself with the cue ball angles.

Speed of cue ball

Notice also the relative distances travelled by the cue ball and object ball after impact. With full-ball contact, the cue ball follows the object ball at less speed and won't travel so far. When playing a fine cut, the cue ball will lose very little of its speed on contact, while imparting less to the object ball. You'll see that if you pot the blue from its spot into the centre pocket with a quarter-ball contact, the cue ball (having been in the bottom half of the table) will have to be played at a speed which will take it to the top cushion and some of the way back again.

Angles around the table

It's not only in potting that you need to know the angles. You'll also negotiate snookers better if you know the angles that the cue ball will come off one or more cushions.

Some are obvious, such as a ball played

Right: Some natural angles around the black showing the paths the cue ball will take after plain-ball pots at full-ball (1), three-quarter ball (2 and 3), half-ball (4 and 5) and quarter-ball (6 and 7).

from the jaws of one baulk pocket to the centre of the top cushion finishing in the other baulk pocket, but others are more subtle. For example, a ball played from the centre of the baulk cushion to the side cushion, half way between the baulk and middle pockets, will cross the table over the blue spot to hit the opposite side cushion midway between middle and top pockets.

Incidentally, get to be able to judge the mid-point between the middle and baulk pockets: it's about 7 inches (18cm) above the baulk line. Midway between the middle and top pockets is level with the pink spot.

Get to know the angle on the opposite cushion between this point on the side cushion 7 inches (18cm) above the baulk line and the top pocket on the same side. To send the cue ball into the top pocket without side you will need to hit the opposite side cushion about 14 inches (35cm) above the middle pocket.

An interesting angle can be found by placing the cue ball on the baulk line between the yellow and brown spots and playing it with right-hand running side towards the left-hand side cushion to make contact about 18 inches (45cm) below the top pocket. If you hit the right spot the ball will hit the top cushion, the right-hand side cushion just below the middle pocket, the baulk cushion near the centre, the left-hand side cushion just below the middle pocket, and go into the top right-hand pocket. Practise this. It is amazing how many times it will help you negotiate snookers.

The right occasions to play shots exactly like those described might occur rarely, but if you practise them you'll become familiar with these angles and be able to adapt them to different positions. You can vary them by hitting the side cushions a little to one side or the other, and of course widen or narrow the angles with side. Even when the cue ball is to hit two or three cushions you'll be able to assess its path.

THORBURN'S TIP

● *Draw a snooker table on a piece of paper and draw in the path of a snooker ball. When it hits the cushion allow it to leave at a right angle. Even if it hits ten cushions, the paths it takes are parallel or at right angles to each other. You can then plot the paths of multi-cushion shots.*

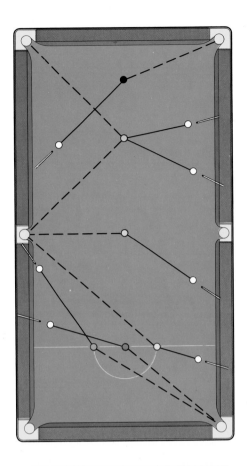

Left: Half-ball pots on the colours from their spots. Practise these and note the angles the cue ball takes.

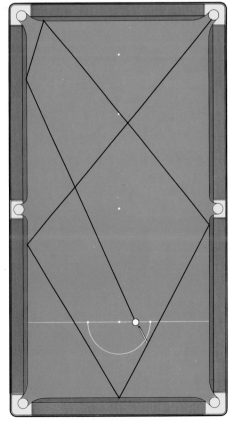

Practise sending the cue ball into the top pocket from the baulk line off five cushions. Right-hand side is required. Try it from other positions on the baulk line.

CHOICE OF SHOT

❛ Do you think some players are consistently luckier than other players? I suggest this 'luck' is based on those players being better at choosing the right shot than others. They know which shots pay the bigger dividends when they work or are less likely to leave an opponent an opportunity when they fail.❜

Choosing the correct shot is one aspect of the game which makes a great difference at all levels. Frequently you see a game between two players of equal skill in shot-making decided not by the run of the balls but because one player consistently chooses a shot which seems to work out well for him. I think the very good player has a feel for the game which is a little like that of a chess player – he can see in advance what might happen if the game develops in a certain way. Sometimes it's a question of just being aware of the possibilities.

A simple example is the situation near the start of a frame where a safety duel is developing, with both players returning to baulk from a split cluster of reds. Often the reds get pushed to one side of the table with both players making thin contacts and returning to baulk, with both, of course, on the lookout for the shot to nothing.

It's the more alert player, however, who

spots the alternative safety shot possibility, and by making a fuller contact on a red brings the cue ball back diagonally across the table from one side cushion to the other to finish in baulk on the opposite side of the table to the reds, thus snookering his opponent on most of the reds behind the line of brown, blue and pink. The pattern is broken, and his opponent has a more awkward shot.

Some shots are so obvious that a better alternative is easily overlooked. If you succeed in the pot in a shot to nothing and come down to baulk without an easy pot of a colour, it's so tempting to trickle up behind the brown, say, that you might do it without noticing the possibility of a green or yellow which has been knocked close to the side cushion. A careful snooker behind one of them might force your opponent to play off the baulk cushion rather than the side, which could make for a much more tricky escape shot.

The state of the score

Sometimes the choice of shot might be between two which look equally sound. The state of the score might decide your choice, and might dictate the more difficult shot.

For example, you have to play a safety shot from near the baulk cushion. There are two reds left, one in the open near the black which gives you an easy return to baulk, the other in a safe position near the side cushion which is slightly more difficult to get safe from. If you're 35 in front, your opponent needs both reds to win, so you will play off the open red and leave the other safe. It ensures that your opponent will probably have to get in twice. Should you be 35 behind, however, you should play off the more difficult red, developing it into the open, so that you can win with one good break.

Of course the principle of knocking balls safe or developing them according to the score is a sound one which isn't confined to playing safety shots. During the course of a break you'll be looking to develop reds if you need them all to win.

Conversely, suppose you are on a break and in attempting to get on the black which

You are 42 in front. Playing the black safe as shown is more likely to ensure a win than playing the cue ball to baulk.

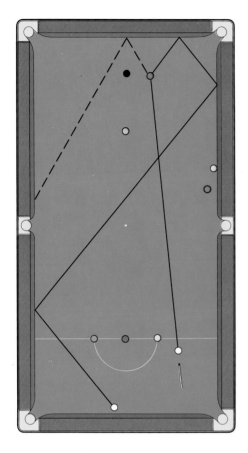

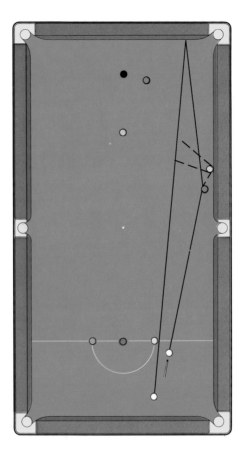

Far left: Here, if 40 in front, play safe off the open red, making it difficult for your opponent to win in one break.

Left: The same position as the previous illustration. If you are 40 behind, play safe off the difficult red, developing both red and blue, making it easier for you to win with one break.

would have made the game 'safe' you misjudge the shot and finish where you can't pot it. You're 42 in front, and there are two reds left at the top of the table. Rather than playing the cue ball safely to the baulk cushion off one of the baulk colours, it might well be better to play the black to the baulk cushion, leaving the cue ball on the top cushion. Unless he gets a snooker, your opponent needs blacks with the two reds to win, and you have now made it much harder for him.

Free ball

The state of the score can be very important when there's only one red left. There are 35 points on the table, but you can still win with one good shot if you are as much as 46 behind. This is because of the free ball rule. If you can lay such a good snooker on the last red that your opponent not only fails to negotiate it, but leaves you a free ball, you have four points for the foul plus the opportunity of another eight for the free ball followed by the black – and you're still in play with the original 35 points still there.

Bear this in mind before potting the second last red. Leave yourself a position on the black so that instead of potting the last red, you can try to lay a difficult snooker with it.

The most profitable free ball I ever had came with four reds left in a match with Jimmy White in the final of the Goya Matchroom Trophy in 1985. Jimmy was 7-0 ahead in the match and 74-0 in the eighth frame when I got the free ball. It put me in control. I took the frame and went on to win the title 12-10. Seventy-four points is more than half the total possible, so Jimmy could feel aggrieved.

A choice of shot which is always tricky is when you're playing from baulk at a red near the top pocket – which, if played with drag, would leave you nicely on the black with, say, four remaining reds invitingly placed. If you get it, a break of 67 is on; if you miss you leave it all for your opponent.

Again, the score might dictate your choice. If you're 60 behind you're unlikely to win without potting all the reds, so even if the odds are slightly against you getting the initial red you should try for it. If you delay, the reds could get knocked safe, and you'd have to make two or three breaks. If you are 60 ahead you might play for safety, concentrating on getting a red or two against the cushion.

CLEARING THE TABLE

' Before I played in tournaments, one practice I found particularly useful was to try to knock the colours in without the cue ball touching a cushion. ,

At the top level, probably about half of snooker frames are undecided by the time the last red disappears, so a player who can sink all the colours will win the frame. The colours are frequently all on their spots, and I would say in that situation the player who gets the yellow clears the table on about 95 per cent of occasions. So the ability to clear the colours from their spots is of paramount importance.

At lower levels of the game the percentage of such clearances is nowhere near so high, but it's clearly a great advantage to be at ease in tackling the colours. On these pages I show a routine way of clearing the colours.

Practise this skill so that whenever you need to clear the table to win you know how to tackle it with confidence.

Remember too that, even in breakbuilding with reds, the colours are potted off their spots more often than not.

You should practise clearing up the colours. If you can do it from the position shown in the first photograph you will win a number of frames on the last 27 points. This is how I set about the colours in the sequence:

Yellow A straightforward plain-ball shot off the right-hand cushion (i.e. right-hand from baulk: left-hand as we look at it) to get on the green;

Green A nearly straight green played with slight screw to hold position on the brown;
Brown A three-quarter ball pot, giving me an easy angle to stun back for the blue;
Blue A simple roll in, the cue ball naturally going on for the pink;
Pink A three-quarter ball pot, with a natural angle to get straight on the black;
Black Straight in – frame and match.

1
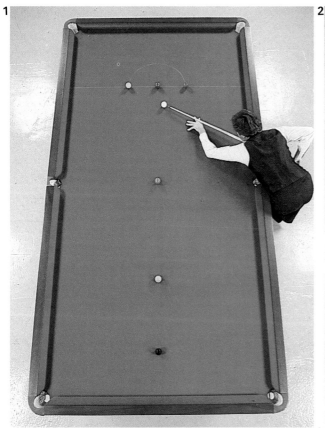

2

3

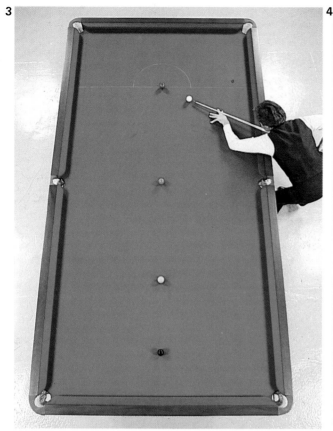

4

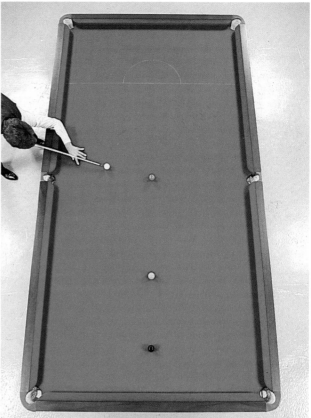

5

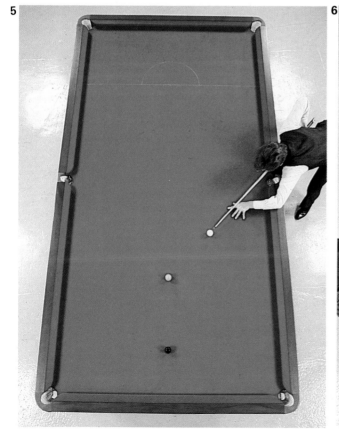

6

MARGIN FOR ERROR

The concept of allowing a margin for error isn't a question of looking for shots where it doesn't matter if you play the shot accurately or not. It's a question of this: where a shot can be played in more than one way, choose the way which is more certain to have the required result.

In making a break, it's much better to have the cue ball travelling towards the next object ball rather than away from it; and, as mentioned in an earlier section, roughly along the line of the next pot rather than across it.

Let's say you've carefully played the cue ball to a position in the baulk half of the table, because there's a red just below the blue, and you have a convenient three-quarter ball pot into the middle pocket to allow you to go up for the pink off its spot, the black being tied up. You need position on the pink so that it's almost a straight pot. You can easily pot the red and stun the cue

ball past the blue to the position you want. The cue ball will take a line towards the top pocket.

However, the ball is running at right angles to the line the pot of the pink will take. You might have a distance of no more than, say, 6 inches (15cm) in which to stop the cue ball. The shot will have to be exact.

The alternative shot, which gives more margin for error, is to pot the red plain ball, running through onto the side cushion with the correct angle to approach the pink. The cue ball can now stop anywhere in a distance of about 2 feet (60cm) and still leave you well on the pink.

Safety in splitting the pack

The angle at which you split the pack can also cut down the possibility of error. Splitting the pack is often a chancy business, but you should always examine it closely to see if there are ways in which you can reduce the chance element. It often happens that a red at the top of the pack is easily pottable if only an adjacent ball can be removed – perhaps even if the awkward ball can be replaced by the cue ball. With a good angle on the black it's sometimes possible to choose your spot in entering the pack. If you can shift the awkward red and leave yourself on the one into the corner, you've played a much better shot than the speculative splitting of the pack.

Beware of reds on the cushion

When playing from baulk towards split reds, intending to bring the ball back to the safety of the bottom cushion, beware reds which might have been pushed to the side cushion, level with the cluster. Often reds get pushed to the left-hand cushion, as most players break-off to the right of the pack.

If the cue ball is down somewhere behind the green, and you intend to play 'thin' off the cluster to the top cushion, you must either play thinly enough to come straight back, or go round the reds near the side cushion.

In the section on snookers I pointed out that if the object ball is near the cushion it presents a bigger target. From the right direction the shot can be off-target by quite

With black tied up, there are two reds which allow getting on to the pink into the middle pocket. Shot 1 is the easier pot, but the cue ball comes down the table across the line of the pot of the pink. Shot 2 brings the cue ball on the line of pot of the pink and is preferable.

a wide margin, but still make contact off the cushion. Similarly, in playing for safety as described, the shot has to be very precise to avoid the reds. Don't try it if the margin for error is so small. If it's impossible to come straight back off the top cushion, or off the other side of the cluster, just to roll up to it.

A safety shot which is often required entails putting the object ball and the cue ball on opposite cushions. It is often played several times when the game is on a re-spotted black.

When playing the object ball from near to a side cushion to the top cushion, it's worth realizing that a double gives you a bigger margin for error. If the object ball is level with the pink spot, one choice would be to play it off the side cushion to the centre of the top cushion, the cue ball meanwhile hitting the top cushion near a pocket and coming back to baulk. If you misjudge the speed or direction of the object ball it could easily finish as a chance of a pot into the top pocket.

There's more margin for error in the double, aiming to bring the object ball across the table to hit the opposite side cushion and thus on to the top cushion. The ball now approaches the top cushion at a much narrower angle, and should therefore stay nearer to it.

The same principle applies when playing the cue ball to the cushion: doubling it should give a better result. The illustration on page 73, of doubling the cue ball off the green onto the top cushion is a good example of this principle. The cue ball, with a fuller contact, could be played to the same position off the left-hand cushion only, but it would approach the cushion at a much fuller angle, and if played too firmly would rebound a long way. By using two cushions, as shown, you make the cue ball approach the cushion at a narrow angle, giving more margin for error.

THORBURN'S TIP

● *Don't allow the consideration of a margin for error to lead you into playing tentatively, as if you need not worry about accuracy. You must still play positively and with the conviction that the shot will turn out as planned.*

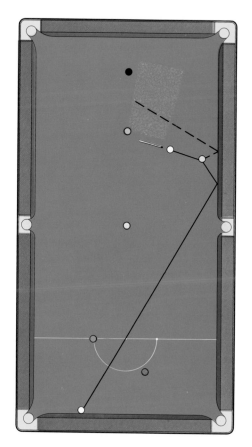

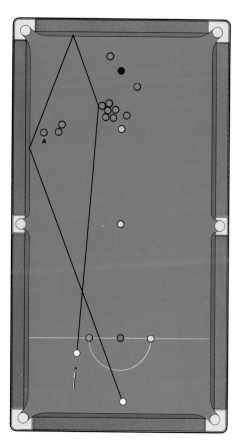

Far left: A good opportunity to lay a snooker. If the cue ball can be placed on the cushion behind the green and blue, there is quite a wide area for the yellow to stop in to effect a snooker.

Left: Without the red marked A the safety shot shown would have plenty of margin for error, but with that red there it is a risky shot. Two other things you could do are to try to pot the red marked A, screwing back for a baulk colour, or to trickle into the reds above the pink, which is also a difficult shot.

NAP OF THE CLOTH

The cloth on a snooker table is made from finest quality wool, and the manufacturers tend to guard closley the secret of its blending. It has a very pronounced nap, which you can feel if you run your hand up and down the cloth. The nap always runs from the baulk end of the table to the top end.

Snooker tables should be regularly ironed. Those used in the professional championships are carefully ironed every day, from baulk upwards. Unfortunately for snooker players the nap has a very pronounced effect on the way the balls run.

The most startling effect can easily be demonstrated by trying swerve shots from both ends of the table. From the baulk end, left-hand side will swerve the cue ball to the left (after the initial push to the right has been nullified), while right-hand side will swerve the ball to the right. From the black spot end of the table, the initial push to one side will never be nullified. A shot played with left-hand side will swerve to the right, and vice-versa. This effect is called *drift*.

Imagine the nap exaggerated, perhaps more like a cat's back. Stroking a cat from head to tail, your hand slides smoothly, but stroking the other way it raises the hairs and meets a lot of resistance. This happens to a snooker ball, although much less noticeably of course. It tends to slow and drift off course as it struggles against the nap, drifting towards the side cushion. A ball directed slowly from the top left-hand pocket to the bottom right will tend to hit the side cushion just above the pocket.

A ball played diagonally towards the bottom left-hand pocket will also fall away towards the side cushion. In other words the ball swerves slightly away from the centre of the table towards the side cushion.

Using the nap

Most players prefer to pot up the table rather than towards baulk, but there are occasions when you can make this drift work for you.

For example, imagine the object ball half way between the pink spot and the side cushion, and you attempting to pot it into the nearest middle pocket. It's a narrow angle. It's practically certain the ball will not drop if it touches the near jaw, and the drift will tend to pull it towards the near jaw. You must play the ball slowly at the far jaw of the pocket, using the slight swerve to curl it in just sufficiently for it to drop after hitting the cushion in the jaw.

The effect of the nap. Notice that the swerve shot B played down the table with left-hand side is not the mirror image of A, the same shot played up the table. Shots D, E, F and G show, in an exaggerated way, the drift which occurs with even plain-ball striking.

THORBURN'S TIP

● *I was playing for $100 a frame in Canada before I knew anything about the nap. When things happened like the pink drifting into the near jaw of the middle pocket most Canadian players thought the table had bad rolls. A friend Jack Pfeffer eventually told me all about it. Canadian tables did not have a strong nap. When I came to Britain I found the nap so strong that it was a new ball game. British and Canadian tables are more alike now.*

BREAKBUILDING SHOTS

In the compilation of a big break, it sometimes becomes necessary to improvise, to play a sort of connecting shot, to get you into position or to regain position if a shot has gone slightly awry. In this section I've identified a few shots which seem to me to crop up more than you would expect.

Often the first shot of a potential break is the trickiest and the most vital. We've dealt with the breaking-off shot, and when and how to split the reds, and we've identified the shot to nothing. But sometimes the opportunity arises to pot the first red in a situation where you can be aggressive.

Imagine there's a loose red about 12 inches (30cm) from the left-hand side cushion, level with the pink spot, while the cue ball is just below the baulk line, near the green. You have a three-quarter ball pot into the top pocket.

There's another red behind the cluster, near the black, which will go into either pocket. In this situation I think the pottable red is too far from the pocket to use a drag shot with the object of staying on the black, and there's the certainty of putting your opponent in if you miss the pot. The shot to play is a firm one, striking the cue ball just above centre to run through and come back off the top cushion to just below the blue. The baulk colours are an insurance against being slightly too strong. Practise this shot.

The pink into the middle pocket is a vital shot, sometimes with a big break as the prize, when the intended red-black sequence hits a snag. Perhaps you have come just too far off the top cushion, and a red is blocking the intended pot of the black to the top pocket. However, the pink is on its spot, and you can continue your break if you can pot it into the middle pocket. It helps your confidence if you've practised potting the pink into the middle pockets at various angles from full-ball to quarter-ball contact.

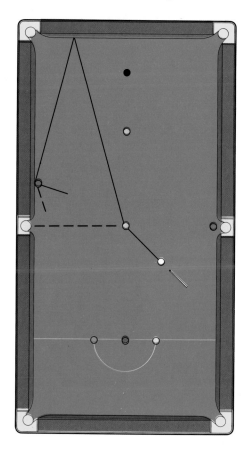

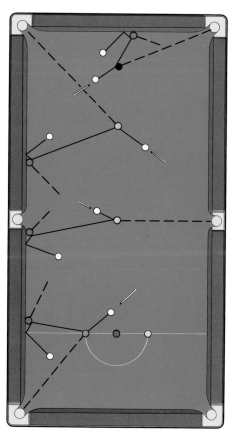

Far left: When potting this blue, it is worth trying to nudge out the red from the cushion. The other red is an insurance against things going wrong. If you pot this red first, there is no insurance when you try to nudge out the last red.

Left: Some examples of nudging reds out from cushions. In each case a chance to pot the red has been created.

Note balls which are potentially in awkward positions and keep on the lookout for opportunities to develop them as the break proceeds. Often this can be done without risk of losing position, and the more pottable balls there are on the table the easier it is to keep the break going.

Nudging out reds

Nudging out reds from the cluster one or two at a time is often more profitable than the more powerful and optimistic splitting of the pack, where you're never sure that it will split very favourably. Often you'll find yourself picking a red off from the edge of the cluster with the angle and opportunity to nudge out another red, but without losing position on the black. Be aware of this possibility, which can be very useful, as nudging one red into position frequently clears the way for another. Set up some practice situations, and see what you can develop. Little screw and stun shots come into their own in these positions.

Nudging balls from a cushion was mentioned in an earlier section. In the close work around the black which is usually the basis of a big break, it's often possible not just to nudge the ball out, but to nudge it towards the pocket. Suppose a red is just off the top cushion above the black, where you can disturb it while potting the black. Aim to hit the red about quarter-ball, so that both red and cue ball hit the top cushion and come away invitingly for the next pot.

Sometimes the black won't pot into either pocket. In these situations a nudge of the black off its spot can turn out well. If you have the angle, a little careful cannon on to the black can nudge the black those 3 or 4

inches (8-10cm) which allow it to be potted.

Cannons on to other balls in the congested area around the black can also be most useful in stopping the cue ball where you want it for the next shot. Set up situations where you can use cannons in this way around the black spot, and practise them.

Potting off the cushion

A shot which can make the difference between continuing a break or running for safety is the pot of a red which is over the pocket but on which you're snookered. In these situations it's often advisable to play this red, because otherwise it's difficult not to leave it for your opponent. Of course, if you've practised potting such balls off the cushion, you'll be much more confident in taking the pot on. The pot is usually a

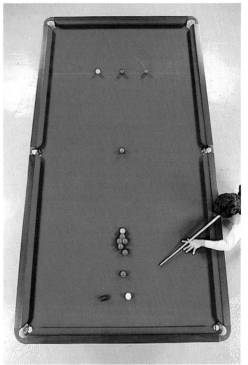

question of hitting the right spot on the cushion. With practice, you'll become familiar with the angles off the cushion to pot these balls. Sometimes you will have to play with running side.

One pot that's often necessary to get a break started, or to prevent one coming to an end, is the long pot of a red, or perhaps the pink off its spot, into a baulk pocket, stunning the cue ball to remain at the top end of the table. Practise these from all

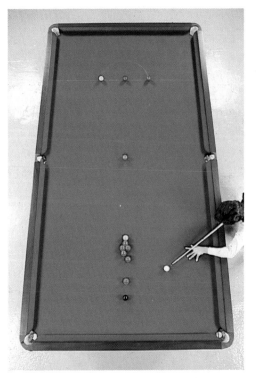

There are two shots in this sequence. Note the position in the first picture. It is easy to roll the black in and get on the red nearest to it. But for breakbuilding I am more interested in the red at the top of the cluster, which will pot only into the top pocket on the other side of the table. In the next two photographs you can see how with a little screw I have got onto this red at an angle to split the pack.

positions near the top of the table. The pot has to be played quite hard, so that there is less chance of the nap of the cloth forcing the object ball off-line.

Getting on the yellow

As we noted earlier, match-winning breaks are frequently required to continue after the

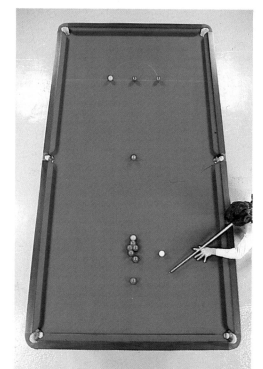

last red has disappeared, and to take in at least a few of the colours. Sometimes you can make the transfer from the top end of the table to the baulk end a little easier by potting the last red for position just above the blue, or even one of the baulk colours,

---

THORBURN'S TIP

● *My friend Willie Thorne is often described as one of the best breakbuilders in the game. What does this mean? Many other players can control the cue ball as well, and pot as well as him. Willie's strength is in seeing the connection from one shot to another. This might be partly instinct, but I'm sure everybody can improve their perception of the direction of a break by studying what happens in certain situations. Perhaps watching Willie would be a good way to start.*

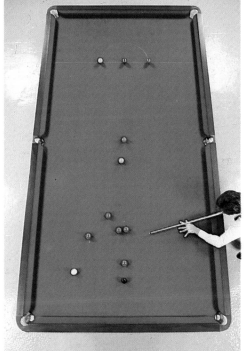

From the shot in the previous three photographs, I can now pot the red as shown and split the pack. If it looks as if the cue ball will be jammed into the reds, a little left-hand side will help throw it clear. Notice the result of the shot. I should now clear the table, a chance I might not have had if I had taken the easy, loose red first.

but often you'll want to get on the yellow from the black off its spot, or the pink into the middle pocket. So practise potting black and pink off their spots from a variety of positions above the pink spot, running down for the yellow in each case. You will usually need to use spin.

PRACTICE AND RHYTHM

I am using a practice routine which most players use in some form or other. With the colours on their spots, and the reds in a line as shown in the first picture, the object is to make as big a break as I can, potting red and colour alternately as in an actual frame, respotting the colours as usual.

The sequence shows me potting the first two reds with a black and pink. The line of balls, by the way, must not be disturbed. If it is, or if you miss a pot, you must start again.

Practice is essential for any player aiming at a respectable level. Every professional practises, and you could almost say, paradoxically, that practice becomes more important the higher in the game you go.

There is, however, a vast difference between good, constructive practice, and going through the motions in order to get in the two hours a day or whatever it is that you've decided is what you need or can spare.

When you practise, you should have some idea of what it is you are practising – and why. And you should always be learning. There's little point in practising a shot ten times and missing it eight times unless you're discovering why you're missing it, and how you can put it right. After all, unless you find these things out, all you're practising is how to *miss* the shot.

A big danger of practice is becoming jaded. When you're practising on your own,

you aren't having the rest between breaks that you'd usually have in a match. One hour's intensive practice might entail as much effort and shot-making as four or five frames in a match, and it's all continuous. Also, you're picking balls out of pockets and replacing them on the table all the time, so it's not surprising if you become bored or even tired. Don't be disappointed if this happens, and don't force yourself to carry on. Give yourself a break: five minutes' practising when you're keen is worth half an hour when you're not.

Practising your cueing action
Playing over the spots up and down the table was suggested as a good practice to determine if your cueing action is all right. But it is boring, so don't spend too long on this sort of exercise. Instead practise straight pots of balls off the blue spot into the top pockets from the baulk line, which tells you

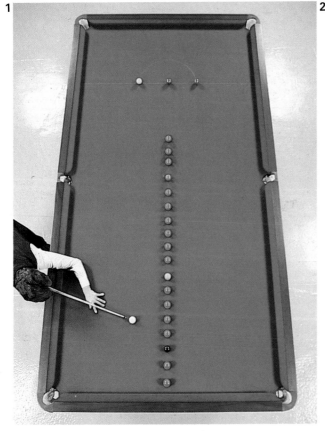

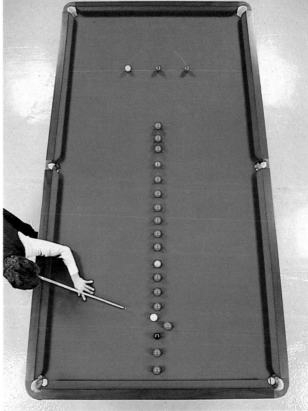

3

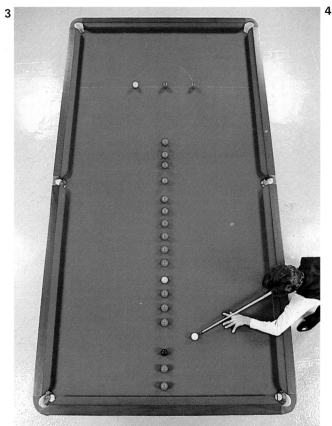

4

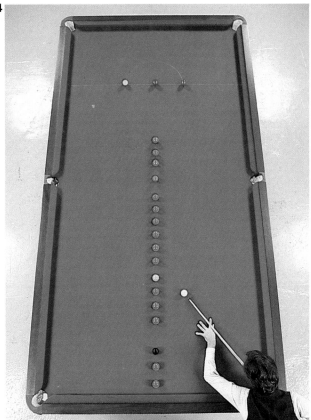

5

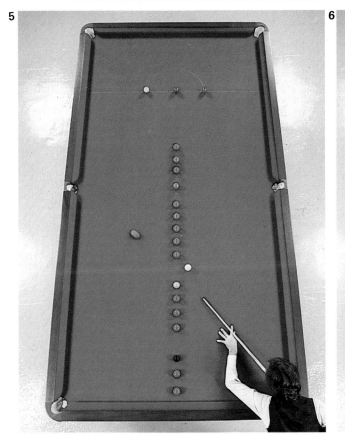

6

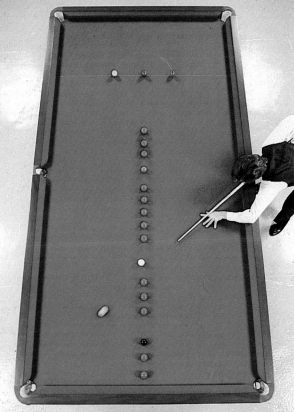

Below: Another practice is to line up five reds as shown and to pot them one at a time, starting with the cue ball on the baulk line. I do this exercise 20 times, and my current standard is to succeed with 16 out of 20.

Below, centre two photographs: I practise doubles by lining up five reds as shown and doubling them one at a time into the middle pocket, taking the cue ball back each time. I stay at this exercise until I have potted all five in one sequence.

much the same thing about your action.

Many suggestions for practice have already been made in the various sections in this book. Some practice set-ups are quite well-known and are used by many players. One is to line up all 21 object balls between the brown and pink spots. Beginning with the cue ball wherever you like, see how many balls you can pot in any order, the only restriction being that you mustn't disturb any other balls in the line. This is a routine that you can practise two or three times in a session, and it has the advantage that you can keep a record of the most balls you potted before it breaks down.

This score-keeping has two invaluable functions. First, if you're trying to beat something, it brings an interest to the practice, leading you to concentrate more and retain your enthusiasm. Second, as you improve you'll beat your record, and this gives you clear evidence of the progress you're making and spurs you on further.

Finding a rhythm

Most players who have been at the game for a number of years seem to develop a playing rhythm. The sort of practice (like the last one mentioned) where you can make a 'break'

without stopping to reset the balls, allows you to find your own rhythm. It's not something you should be conscious of — it should come naturally. If you get to the top, others will make comments about how fast or slow your tempo is, but that's no reason for changing it. I mention it here just so that you can be aware of it. If, for example, you should realize that you missed a shot because you weren't quite settled and comfortable, or hadn't given it enough thought, take a little more time. Conversely, if you feel you missed a shot because you fiddled around too much, try the effect of speeding up a little. I emphasize, however, that you shouldn't be self-conscious about rhythm. The one you drop into naturally is probably the best for you.

No matter how well you practise, don't forget that the object of it all is to enable you to win matches. So play as many matches and enter as many tournaments as you can. Try to play a wide variety of opponents, not only so that you meet many other styles, but also so that you play opponents of many temperaments. When you're so used to playing strangers that the opposition all comes as one to you, then you'll be able to play your natural game.

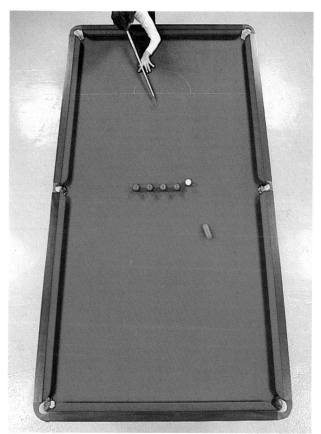

While you're still forming and polishing your game, always try to win, of course, but don't be afraid of taking a chance and trying your shots. If you can play a shot in practice, don't be scared to play it in a match because you might miss and give away the frame.

Don't worry if such tactics lose you a match or two. Put it down to experience, and look forward to when you'll reverse the result.

I still practise, and find it's very necessary. On these pages I've outlined a few of the routines I sometimes follow.

THORBURN'S TIPS

● *I feel strongly that you should regard actual matches as practice until you get to tournament-winning standard. There is a tendency among beginners to play matches as if each should be won at all costs, so they do not play shots they're not 100 per cent sure of. It is trying and succeeding with these shots in matches that brings the confidence to use them again until they become part of your normal repertoire. To use an expression: Go for it. You'll get it in the end.*

● *When practising, spend a little time on all aspects of the game – long potting, fine cuts, getting the cue ball on the bottom cushion, etc – because this will keep your game 'well-oiled'*

and in working order. But also isolate your weaknesses and have special sessions to practise them. The application of a little simple intelligence is essential. You must identify why you miss certain shots. So study what happens when you miss, experiment, get it right and iron out a weakness.

● *Make a little private game of practice. If you have a few favourite set routines, devise a way of keeping score while you practise. For example, if you practise potting blue and black from their spots, as in the illustration on page 27, note how many pots you make in one round (maximum 16). Watching your form fluctuate and gradually improve will give you interest and enthusiasm. Eventually you will regularly score 16, when you will find more interest in a more difficult routine.*

Below: Practising long pots. With the cue ball between the yellow spot and the cushion the first pot is a straight red. The second is a half-ball pot which I practise from the brown spot with left-hand side to send the cue ball swinging behind the black spot and back to baulk, between the pink and blue spots. These practices are my last before a tournament, as these pots come early in a game.

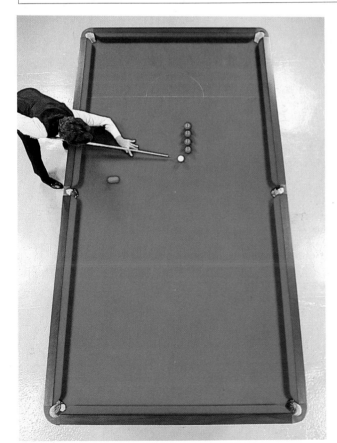

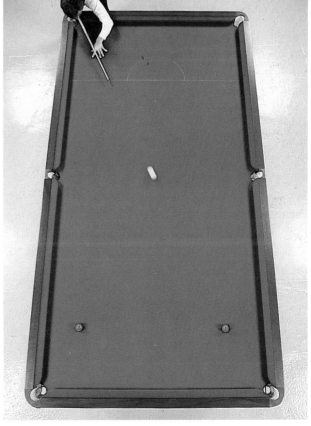

TRICK SHOTS

❛ Some people can make snooker balls behave in a most extraordinary way. Spectacular trick shots are great entertainment, but don't get carried away – in a snooker match there are no marks for artistic impression. ❜

Nearly all professional players give exhibitions, and include a few trick shots in their repertoire. Trick shots, properly regarded, can help in practice and provide entertainment, and they have a useful place on the snooker scene. There's a danger that some budding players get so taken with their prowess at trick shots that they think these shots are more important than the game itself – but I'm sure you're not among them!

Some trick shots use props – baskets, bottles or members of the audience. However, what are most useful for the player learning the skills of the game are those shots which are called trick shots, but aren't really tricks at all. They might be spectacular effects, but no more skill is needed than the good player possesses, and the balls don't behave in any extraordinary way. They might not behave as the uninitiated expect, but they obey the natural laws, and the expert isn't surprised.

Studying what happens to the balls in these shots can tell the young player or the beginner a lot about the game, and if nobody actually duplicates them in a match, at least they have the value of showing what is possible.

Some trick shots are just intended to amuse. Here's one you can try. Place a red in the jaws of each baulk pocket and lay two cues across the table so that the tips are touching the reds, the butts overlapping at the centre of the table just off the baulk cushion. The set-up is such that a ball hitting the overlapping butts will knock the two reds into the pockets. Place the cue ball on the brown spot and announce that you will pocket three balls with one shot. Play hard up the table and as the cue ball comes back and hits the butts it will knock in the two reds and jump over the bottom rail, where you are ready to catch it and slip it instantly into your pocket.

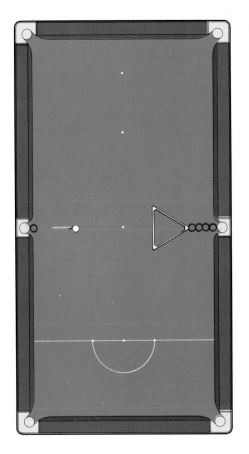

On the left side is the set-up for my first 'trick' shot. I propose to pot all five reds in one shot. The secret is to strike the cue ball on the centre line between 12 o'clock and 6 o'clock (i.e. without side), but just below the centre spot (i.e. with slight backspin). In the sequence you can see it happening and, as a bonus, the cue ball disappears as well.

1

2

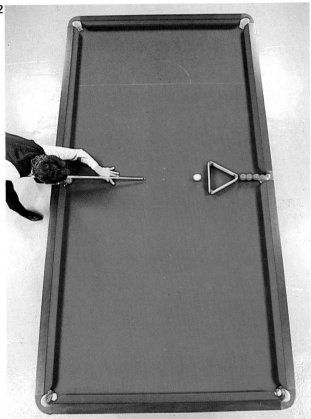

3

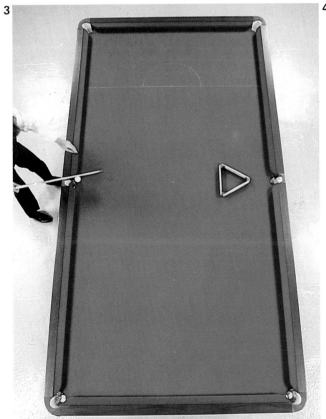

4

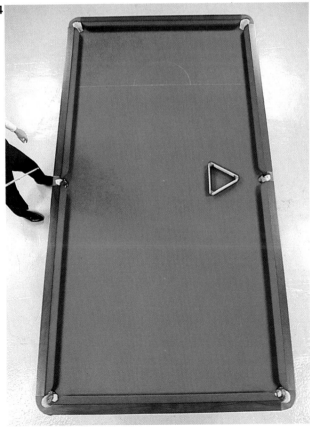

On this and the previous page I've played a couple of shots that audiences seem to like in my routine, and with a little practice you should be able to perform them yourself. Both use the triangle and in fact neither is difficult. I hope you enjoy them, but don't regard them as ends in themselves. The play's the thing, not the tricks.

The reds are set up in their usual pyramid inside the triangle, but the red near the pink spot is taken away, and the cue ball is placed as shown, with the triangle resting on it. The red is placed beside the triangle, and I am going to play it off three cushions so that it ends up in its place in the pyramid and enclosed by the triangle.

The sequence shows where contact is made with the cushions, and the red coming into the pack and dislodging the white, whereupon the triangle drops neatly over it.

1

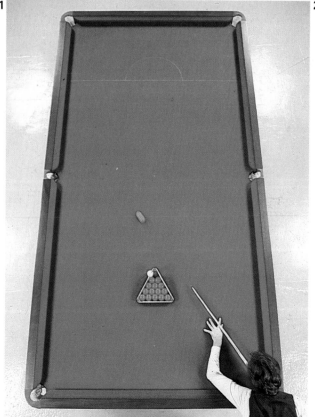

2

3

4
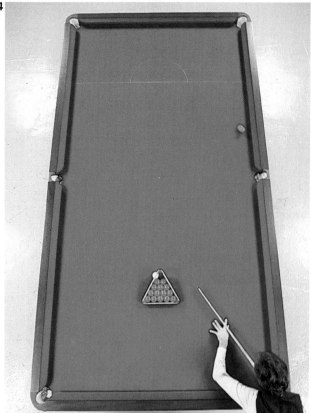

5
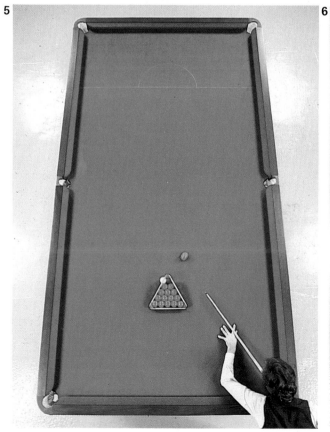

6
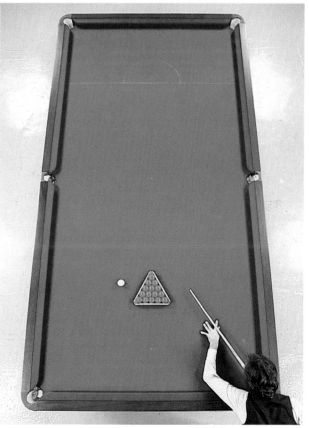

IT'S ALL IN THE MIND

> ❝ The more you study the game the more you'll enjoy it and the more you'll get wrapped up in the tactical battle going on on the table. And the more your brain is involved in the game, the less it is worrying about your nerves. ❞

> ❝ If things aren't going right and you feel bad or nervous, don't sit worrying while your opponent is at the table. Counting from one to twenty in your head might steady you down. The point is it's better to think of nothing at all than to think negative thoughts. Sometimes I've found it necessary to count to 200 to get back into the right frame of mind. ❞

Snooker is a fascinating game because it has so many facets. You need, first of all, technical ability, which in itself has many aspects: some players are good potters, others excel at cue ball control; you need an awareness of the game, a sort of 'snooker sense' to help you to choose the right shot at any particular time; you need a more general idea of tactics – how to maximize your own potential and put your opponent under pressure; and you need the right temperament – the ability to be able to concentrate and give of your best without the inhibitions that come from nervousness and awe of the big occasion.

This last one, your mental attitude during a game, is probably as important in snooker as in any game. In reaction sports like tennis and soccer, the nerves a player has before a match tend to evaporate as soon as the action starts. A tennis player facing a Boris Becker service has almost no time for nerves: he gets into position and plays his shot instinctively. All his learning has been done for years previously and he now reacts. If he had to think about the position of his feet and the technique of putting racquet to ball, the ball would be past him without his making a shot.

In snooker it's not like that – and nor is it in another of my favourite pastimes, golf. We players have all the time in the world to worry about what we're doing! No sooner do we think of our bridge than it slips or of our cueing action than it wobbles.

Why does this happen, and how can we prevent it happening? After all, we play all the shots in practice, so how can we play them in a match in the same way? The answer, of course, is to relax – and that's no answer at all. The point is then, how can we relax?

The overall picture
The first thing to realize is that everybody suffers from nerves of this sort to some degree, and that they're not entirely destructive. They get the adrenalin running, they hype you up and can inspire you. Think of the reverse – that the big matches made no impression on you at all. Now that really would be a cause for worry!

Nowadays I'm sometimes described as nerveless – a player who not only relishes the drawn-out struggle but who's usually a reasonable bet to win in the final frame if it gets that far. But not only is this untrue, but a few years ago could be seen to be untrue. When I was achieving a reasonable proficiency at snooker, I'd get so nervous in a long break that after reaching 50 I'd be forced to have a drink or wipe my cue in order to compose myself. Readers might remember that I did a similar thing during my world championship 147 at The Crucible.

One thing which helped me I've mentioned earlier. I developed the technique of looking at the shot and myself dispassionately from the outside, so that I could play the shot as if I were watching me playing it rather than actually going through the motions myself. This ironed out the tendency to start fussing about on the shot, which is the result of nerves.

Later I read *Zen in the Art of Archery* (see page 20) and was impressed by the stage further which that book revealed in the process, whereby the ball, cue, table, pocket and player all become one, and the ball gets potted without the player being aware of taking aim.

All this, of course, is very advanced philosophy, but it has its basis in a simple proposition which might help any player suffering from nerves at the vital moments: the idea of eliminating the ego. If you can realize that making your first 50 break, or even 100 break, is no great occasion, that winning your first tournament of this or that importance does not change the world, that all you can do is to play your best, and that that is simple, you will find that relaxation comes.

Playing at a natural speed
What happens to many players at a vital moment is that in an effort to take more care, they take longer over the shot. This gives more time for things to go wrong. Then, if they miss a few vital shots, they go to the other extreme – to get the ordeal over, they speed up their usual pace.

This indicates the value of developing a natural rhythm at which to play. If you refuse

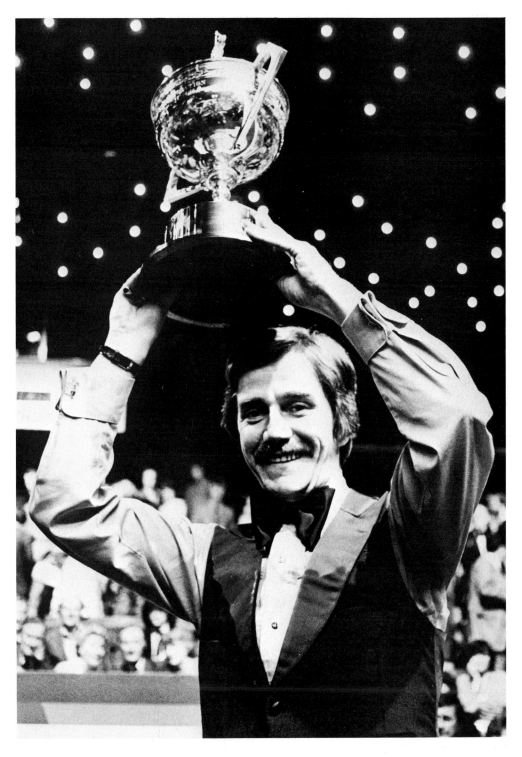

The large bow tie and wide lapels date this photograph to 1980 – as does the world championship trophy.

to deviate from it by not admitting that one shot is intrinsically different from another you'll be on the way to playing your 'natural game'. This isn't to deny, of course, that some situations require more thought in the choice of shot than others. It means that when you've decided on the shot you must play it normally.

In a way, if you're a player on your way up, you're in an enviable position regarding mental attitude. After all, it really doesn't matter if you're beaten – it's all experience in your progress upwards. All you have to do is play your game. You have nothing to lose. You have my permission to start having nerves when you get to The Crucible.

❛ Although my 147 break seemed to come from nowhere, I had seen it happen so many times in my mind – and had actually dreamt about it. In the same way it helps you to win if you have visualized yourself winning in advance. But also realize that you can't win every time, just as I don't make 147 every time. Don't be too disappointed when you lose. ❜

Always be neat, comfortable and prepared mentally and physically to do your best.

MATCH PREPARATION

How do you get ready for a tournament, or even a match? Do you make any special preparations, or do you just turn up at the appointed time and get on with it?

These occasions are ideal opportunities for you to measure your progress, and you should regard them as chances to put into practice what you've learned.

While you're developing your game you should look on matches as stepping stones. Don't be depressed if you lose, but treat them seriously.

First of all, make sure that your cue and especially your tip are in good order. This is trickier than it sounds, for a tip can take a few weeks to wear itself in, and nobody likes to play with a new one. It takes a little while to get used to it. On the other hand, after perhaps months of being absolutely satisfied with your tip, you'll find that suddenly it's become hard and shiny and unwilling to take the chalk. If you detect the beginning of this deterioration, it's better to change your tip in time to give yourself a chance to get used to the new one before your big match.

Professionals have troubles with their tips. It's unavoidable with so many tournaments during the season. I had plenty of tip trouble in the final of the BCE International at Stoke in 1986, and had to request a 15-minute time-out to change my tip in the final session. I lost, having led.

Make sure you have your chalk with you when you leave for the match, and use it well. No harm is done if you chalk your cue every other stroke, and certainly chalk it before each spin shot. But remember, it's just a light wipe; don't grind the chalk in.

Dress is important. Find out in advance if there are any dress requirements for the tournament – for example if ties are required or jeans are banned. Whether there are or not, dress neatly and comfortably. The same thing goes for personal grooming. If your hair is going to fall into your eyes every time you get down for a shot, then do something about it. The object is to be satisfied with your appearance, and not to be flamboyant or conspicuous. Then you can forget all about it, and concentrate on your game.

Shoes are the most important part of dress. You must be comfortable in them, as you are going to be standing and walking round the table quite a lot. Don't wear shoes which will embarrass you by squeaking, or pinch your corn so that half your mind is thinking of the pain and the other half of the pot.

Relaxation is preparation

Try to get a period of relaxation at home before leaving for the match. If you have to dash home from work, say, grab a meal and leave, then you must, but it's not the best preparation. Relaxing at home is the best order of the day – far better than hanging around at the venue waiting for things to start.

On the other hand, of course, you must arrive in plenty of time, and without having hurried. Dashing to the venue, fearing you'll be late, and turning up flustered is the worst preparation of all. The object is to start with a relaxed body and a mind ready to concentrate on the game.

Concentrate from the very first shot, and take care on every stroke. Do not begin with a preconceived notion of how you'll play. Keep your tactics flexible, and think of how the game is going. If you feel you're on a good streak, go for your shots. If, on the other hand, your opponent is on a good streak, try to break up his tempo. Don't concede a frame too hastily if you can keep him on the table for a while with some safety play. Perhaps his touch will desert him before the next frame.

Don't react to any luck your opponent might have, and take any you have impassively. Don't chat to opponents or spectators. Some matches, of course, are very informal, and behaving as if they were the world championship final would appear ridiculous, but treating everybody politely and erring on the side of formality isn't a bad habit to acquire.

I do not want to ban personality. I make occasional remarks in the most serious matches. But *never* risk putting off your opponent.

Above all, try to enjoy the game. Accept success quietly, and defeat sportingly – and remember that you'll learn more from your defeats.

❝ When playing a match you want to be able to give all your attention to it. This can be achieved by advance planning and attention to detail (e.g. have you a clean handkerchief?) If you arrive cool, comfortable and relaxed, confident that both you and your equipment are in good condition, you will be able to give of your best. ❞

SUMMARY

If you've followed and absorbed the information in this book to this point I'm sure that your game has improved considerably. This summary is intended as a reminder of the most important points. The very basic things are of premier importance, because nobody can succeed without mastering them. They are covered up to page 29 or so.

It's not worth compromising with the basic stroke. Some people do reasonably well with personal unconventional styles, but if you are serious about your game you might just as well practise the approved and accepted techniques. They're known to be good enough to take you as far as you want to go.

Pages 30 to about 67 deal with more advanced techniques. It's essential to master them if you want to become world champion, but you could become a good club player without using them all. From page 68 we have mostly been isolating details which help to polish your game.

From the beginning, buy your own cue. Experiment with club cues, certainly, to discover the weight you prefer. If you're fully grown, I recommend a length so that if stood on the floor the tip should reach 2 or 3 inches (50-75mm) above your armpit. If you're average height, this will be around 4ft 10in (147cm), or a standard length of cue. Look after the cue carefully, and learn how to fit and shape your own tips.

Stance

Grip the cue in the manner recommended; idiosyncratic grips will probably lead to the position of the elbow becoming awkward and the cueing action going astray.

The majority of your shots at the table will be made with the standard bridge and stance, so get the stance correct. Remember how everything lines up in relation to the direction of the shot: feet, cue, wrist, elbow, shoulder, chin.

Every now and then – and particularly if

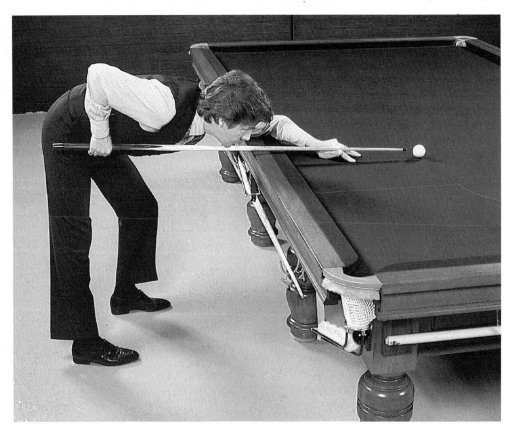

Take another look at the stance and get right all the elements mentioned in the text.

you strike a bad patch – check that your stance is correct. Something out of position could easily mean that the cue is not coming through straight, leading you to miss pots you expect to get, and it's not easy to diagnose the reason unless you keep watch on your basic technique. Don't be misled by the occasional eccentricity you might see among the leading players: Ray Reardon's elbow juts out, but this is due to a shoulder broken when he was learning, and is not the reason for his success!

One problem I have had in writing this book is that my elbow juts out, too, as you can see particularly well in the picture on page 13. So it looks as if I'm saying 'Don't do as I do, do as I say'. The reason for my 'incorrect' stance is a shoulder once thrown out playing baseball. Ray Reardon and I have both overcome our problems in this direction, so obviously one can play well with one aspect of the stance being not as recommended. But – and this is important – if you haven't got as good an excuse as Ray or me, then you are advised to play in the approved classical and correct manner.

Bridge

Bear in mind the purpose of the bridge: it's not just a convenient way to park your non-striking hand and separate the cue from the table. It's essential for your balance, and for supporting the cue so that it travels easily on the line intended. Remember how necessary it is to be firm.

If you can recognize what makes a good bridge, you won't be embarrassed when the cue ball lands in an awkward place: you'll be able to adapt. Observe the various ways you can play up the table when the cue ball is on or near the baulk cushion – a problem you'll have more and more often as your standard improves. And practise the various bridges which straddle the cushion, the ones necessary when you have to play parallel to the cushion.

There's also the high bridge, which you'll need to be able to form when playing over an intervening ball. Be sure that all these bridges are mastered.

Sometimes, of course, a hand bridge will be impossible, and you must use one of the rests – perhaps the half-butt, which also entails lengthening your cue, or using a strange one. Make sure you're at home with the rests. Don't get yourself into a situation where, because you are unhappy using the rest, you're uncertain whether or not to use it for a shot. In such cases, whether you

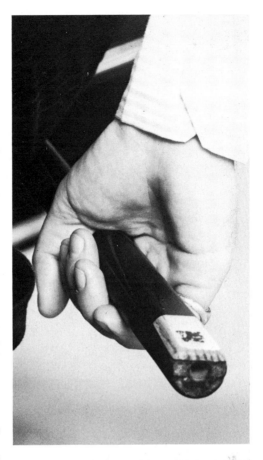

Left: Pay attention to your grip. Let the butt lie across the middle joints of the fingers.

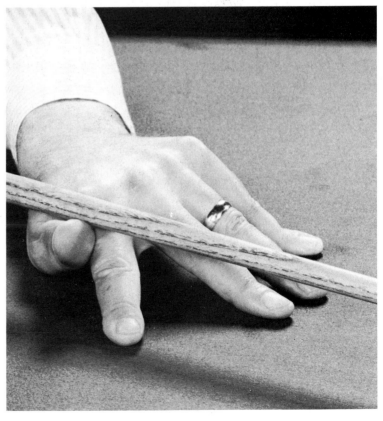

Below: Remember the bridge is very important to your stability. Notice the fingers pressing into the cloth.

Proper practice will prepare you for any situation on the table, and you will negotiate tricky positions even with a referee like Len Ganley peering over your shoulder.

choose to use it or not, if you miss the shot you will brood on it. Just make sure you can use the rest, and relieve yourself of this dilemma.

When sighting the shot, remember the advisability of looking at the object ball at the moment of striking. But don't forget to consider the cue ball as well, and in particular to be certain that the cue is striking it at the spot desired.

Build up a rhythm and routine for feathering before you make the shot. This is something that should become well grooved, so that you won't actually be thinking of it as you do it. It will be a reflex action.

When you finally draw the cue back to make the strike, don't overlook the almost imperceptible pause before you drive the cue forward.

You won't be conscious of making decisions in this fraction of a second, but in fact you'll be drawing everything together ready for the shot. Remember the importance of the follow-through; the need to keep everything except your arm still; the need to resist the temptation of lifting your head; and the general desirability of staying down over the shot.

Spin
Study the various effects that spin has on the behaviour of the cue ball and practise them so that you know exactly what will happen wherever your cue strikes the cue ball.

Screw and stun are absolutely necessary if you want to approach professional standard. Remember the need to lower the bridge for playing with screw, and how it's done.

Side is very complicated, and even some professionals are reluctant to use it too much. You should be aware of its effects, and practise using it, because if you can incorporate it into your game you'll be a far better player.

Remember that your cue will have to be parallel with the line of the shot and that you don't just aim at the side of the cue ball. You should have decided on your shot before you settle into your stance but if you do decide to change your shot after getting into your stance, get up and line the shot up again.

Don't make last-second adjustments.

Master the swerve shot, which is a form of side, and is useful for many situations on the table.

Cue ball control and potting

The ability which sorts out the great snooker players from the others is cue ball control. If you can control the position of the cue ball it will make all the other elements so much easier. So absorb the pages on cue ball control and those on elements of play which largely rely on cue ball control such as safety play, snookering, getting the cue ball back to baulk, and so on.

One shot which involves cue ball control, and which you will have to make in about half the frames you play in, is the breaking-off shot. This is always the same, as no balls have been disturbed, and your opponent cannot influence it at all. It's a vital shot, and there's no excuse for making a mess of it. So make sure you practise it to perfection. Every time you break off you must put your opponent on the defensive.

However good your cue ball control, though, you cannot win games without potting, so get to know all the angles. Practise potting at full-ball round to fine cut, and practise potting while controlling the cue ball with spin. Remember the value of plants. They offer one of the safest pots in the game, so get to know the angles at which the cue ball must contact the object ball.

Don't forget that near-plants can often be potted if you make the right contact, and reverse plants, where the object ball to be potted is the nearer ball. Keep watch for plants when playing matches, as the first player to spot one and take advantage usually gets a few points from it.

Doubles are other pots which can lead to a useful advantage. Sometimes a player is forced to attempt a double, and whether or not he's successful can decide the frame. So practise doubles and be confident when you tackle them in a match.

Test for yourself the effect of the nap of the cloth as described on page 100, and learn how to use it to your advantage.

If you become technically expert, by which I mean you play the strokes correctly, can control the cue ball and spin, can pot the balls, and know the angles, then I'm sure the tactics, and the feel for the game which enables you to make the right selection of shot, will come naturally.

Above all – *practise*. Snooker is a great game, and while you continue to think of it as a great game you'll keep your enthusiasm for it, and practice will be that much easier.

And don't forget it *is* only a game. Take victory and defeat sportingly.

The ultimate success: the Embassy World Professional Snooker Championship Trophy. Keep practising and every day you'll get a little closer to the top.

THORBURN'S TOP TEN TIPS

● *Choose a cue to suit yourself and look after it carefully.*

● *Get the basics right: pay attention to your stance, grip and bridge.*

● *Practise striking the ball and potting from all angles.*

● *Study the effects of spin and practise them.*

● *Practise controlling the cue ball until you can place it where you want.*

● *Watch the great players as often as possible, either live or on television and analyse their techniques.*

● *Ask why professionals choose a certain shot in a certain situation and thus develop a feel for tactics.*

● *Don't be afraid to experiment.*

● *Prepare for your matches so that you can do your best and behave in a sporting manner during them.*

● *Enjoy yourself.*

GLOSSARY

Angled When the cue ball comes to rest in the jaws of a pocket so that a corner of the cushion prevents contact in a straight line with any part of the balls on.

Ball on The ball, or any of the balls, which can legally be hit by the cue ball, i.e. the next ball to be played. It is sometimes said of a ball which it is possible to pot, i.e. 'the blue is on into the middle pocket'.

Baulk The area on the table between the bottom cushion and baulk line.

Break The succession of consecutive shots which a player makes at one turn at the table. Also said of the number of points scored, i.e. 'a break of 30'. The first shot in a frame is sometimes called the 'break-off'.

Bridge The support for the cue formed by the hand which is placed on the table. Also used to describe the distance between the hand forming the bridge and the cue ball.

Check side See Side.

Clearance The potting of all the object balls remaining on the table, i.e. the last break of a frame, which clears the table.

Cluster A group of reds close together, those remaining in a tight group after the pack has been split.

Colour One of six object balls which are not red, i.e. the yellow, green, brown, blue, pink and black.

Cue ball The white ball, struck by the cue.

Cut A fine shot, in which the object ball is contacted on its edge: a 'thin' contact.

D The semi-circle drawn from the yellow to the green spot, and the part of the table enclosed by this semi-circle and the baulk line.

Double A shot in which an object ball is deliberately played against a cushion to travel across the table to an opposite pocket.

Follow-through The action of the cue after the cue ball is struck. The amount by which the cue travels past the original position of the cue ball after striking.

Frame A period of play from the setting up of the balls in their starting positions until the final black is potted or fouled. When one player is eight or more points ahead with only the black left, it is customary not to play the black, since the player behind cannot win. A player who falls so far behind that he is almost certain to lose may concede the frame on his turn.

Free ball If a player is snookered on the ball or balls on after a foul stroke by his opponent, the referee awards a free ball. This allows the player to nominate any other ball to be the ball on. Any ball nominated is given the value of the ball on for that particular stroke, and the break proceeds as normal. The player can, of course, ask his opponent to play again, as after any foul stroke.

Game An agreed number of frames. When a player has won an unbeatable number of frames (e.g. five in a nine-frame game) it is customary not to play the remainder.

In-hand When the cue ball enters a pocket or is forced off the table it is said to be in-hand until it is legally re-introduced to the table and played from the D.

In-off The action of the cue ball entering a pocket after contact with the object ball.

Jump shot A shot in which the cue ball jumps over another ball when struck by the cue, even if the cue ball touches the other ball while jumping it. However, if the cue ball jumps another after impact with an object ball, it is not a jump shot. A jump shot is a foul.

Kick Sometimes after contact, the cue ball or object ball does not behave as expected, e.g. it does not travel in its expected direction. This phenomenon is accompanied by a distinctive sound. Sometimes chalk or dirt on one of the balls is the cause, but in other cases it is a mystery.

Massé An exaggerated swerve shot, played with the butt of the cue raised high, often making the cue vertical.

Match An agreed number of games or frames.

Maximum The maximum break, which is regarded as 147, although it is possible to make a higher break if it starts with a free ball.

Miscue An incorrect striking of the cue ball, which sometimes causes it to jump.

Nap The nap of the cloth, which runs from baulk to top cushion and has an effect on the running of the balls.

Nominated ball The next object ball, which the striker declares, or indicates to the referee's satisfaction, to be the next ball on. A player nomimates the colour he intends to play after potting a red, or after being awarded a free ball.

Object ball The ball to be struck by the cue ball.

Occupied If a colour is potted or forced off the table and cannot be replaced exactly on its own spot because another ball or balls prevent it, then the spot is said to be occupied.

Pack The 15 reds, especially when in their 'triangle' at the beginning of a frame.

Plain-ball striking Hitting the cue ball 'straight', without spin or side.

Plant A shot in which one object ball is played onto another to pot it. A set is frequently also called a plant.

Pot The legal knocking of an object ball into a pocket.

Push stroke When the cue is still in contact with the cue ball when the cue ball makes contact with the object ball, or after the cue ball has begun its forward motion. A push stroke is a foul.

Pyramid spot The spot on which the pink is placed.

Run-through The action of the cue ball after topspin has been applied. It travels further than it would from a plain-ball spot.

Running side See Side.

Safety shot A shot where the intention is not to pot a ball but to make it difficult for the opponent to do so.

Screw The backspin put on to the cue ball which makes it travel backwards after contact with the object ball.

Set The situation of two or more balls touching and in line with a pocket, so that the furthest can be potted by contacting the nearest. Nowadays more usually called a plant.

Shot to nothing A safety shot which also carries the possibility of a pot. Thus the pot, if successful, is a bonus.

Side Sidespin applied to the cue ball to make it swerve, or more usually to alter the angle at which the cue ball will leave a cushion. Side which widens the angle and takes the cue ball further away from its starting point is called *running side*.

Side which narrows the angle is called *check side*.

Snooker When the cue ball cannot be played in a straight line to hit the ball on, or any of the balls on, because another ball or balls are in its path. If no part of the ball or balls on can be hit, it is sometimes called a full snooker, if only a part of the ball or balls on can be hit, it is sometimes called a partial snooker. So far as the rules concerning a free ball are concerned, a partial snooker is regarded as a snooker, and if two or more balls are effecting the snooker, the nearest to the cue ball is regarded as the snookering ball. A cue ball played from in-hand is snookered if it cannot be played in a straight line to the object ball or balls from any part of the D.

Spot, the The spot on which the black ball is placed at the start of the game.

Spot, to To replace a colour on its spot after it has been potted or forced off the table.

Striker The player in play on the table, or the player whose turn it is to play.

Stroke The action of striking the cue ball with the cue, and the period between the striking of the cue ball and the balls coming to rest.

Stun The backspin put onto a cue ball to make it stop dead on contact with the object ball or to travel less far than it would with plain-ball striking.

Topspin The spin put on the cue ball to make it run through further than normal after contact with the object ball.

Touching ball When the cue ball comes to rest so that in the opinion of the referee it is touching a ball on, or a ball which could legitimately be nominated as the ball on. The striker must play away from this ball: otherwise the strike is adjudged a push stroke. He is regarded as having played the ball on.

SOME POINTS IN THE RULES

Snooker players studying this book to improve their game will be familiar with the basic rules of snooker: the order in which the colours are potted, their value, etc. However, there are many rules about which even regular players are not certain. It is not enough to assume that the referee is there for guidance, as the referee is limited in the ways he can intervene. The rules of the Billiards and Snooker Control Council (BSCC) only allow him to answer questions authorized in the rules, and he is not allowed to give advice or express an opinion, nor even to warn a player that a foul is about to take place.

Snooker players will tend to be better players the more they know the game in all its aspects, and a thorough knowledge of these lesser-known rules will bring its own reward in enjoyment.

For example, most players know the standard dimensions of a full-sized snooker table, but how many know the height? As a snooker player will bend over the table several thousand times in his career, its height is important to him. The rules state that the height of the top of the cushion rail from the floor shall be between 2 feet $9\frac{1}{2}$ inches and 2 feet $10\frac{1}{2}$ inches (850 mm and 875 mm).

A resumé of the less well-known rules should begin where the game does – in striking the cue ball.

A stroke in snooker is a fair stroke if it is made with the tip of the cue, and the cue ball is struck once only. If the tip remains in contact with the ball when it has begun its forward motion, this is a push stroke and is a foul. When the cue ball and the object ball are very close together, it can happen that the tip of the cue is still in contact with the cue ball when the object ball is struck. This is also a push stroke. The penalty for a push stroke is the value of the ball struck, provided it is the ball on, and with the proviso that the minimum penalty in snooker is four points.

The calculation of a penalty in snooker is straightforward. It is always the value of the ball on or the ball concerned in the foul (such as a ball illegally potted), whichever is the greater. If more than one foul is committed in the same stroke, the penalty is the higher or highest valued foul. All snooker penalties therefore range between four points (the minimum) and seven (the value of a foul involving the black). If the foul is not classifiable as above (i.e. if the striker uses a red or a colour as the cue ball), the penalty is the maximum of seven points.

A jump shot, when the striker causes the cue ball to jump over any other ball, whether it touches it or not, and whether it is intentional or not, is also now a foul. Thirty years ago instruction books would show the reader how to play a jump shot without ripping the cloth. It is now illegal, but it is not a foul if a ball leaves the bed of the table after contact with the object ball, which occasionally happens, particularly if the shot is played with a lot of spin. (If a ball jumps off the table altogether, it *is* a foul, of course, in any circumstances).

When playing from hand, a player is allowed to use the cue to position the ball in the D, and even if the tip of the cue touches the cue ball, the ball is not regarded as in play, and the referee does not call a foul if he is satisfied that the player was not attempting to play a stroke.

Other fouls which can be committed in the actual striking of the ball include striking when the balls are not at rest, striking the cue ball more than once, striking with both feet off the floor and striking out of turn. All these fouls carry the four-point penalty.

A striker must always attempt to hit the ball on. Without this rule it could be to the advantage of a player to make a deliberate miss. If the referee is satisfied that a true

The referee positions the balls at the start of a frame during a Benson and Hedges Irish Masters match at Goffs, County Kildare. The referee is not allowed to advise players about to break a rule, so all players should have a good working knowledge of the rules.

attempt has not been made to hit the ball on, he must call a miss, award the appropriate penalty (the value of the ball on) and ask the non-striker if he wishes the ball to be replaced and the striker to play again.

A striker need not attempt to hit the object ball full, but he must attempt to hit it, even if it is only to trickle up to the edge of it. It is assumed that professional players do not deliberately try to miss, but sometimes when they leave the ball short the referee will call a miss on the grounds that in his opinion the attempt to hit the ball was not of the standard that he would expect. In a Benson and Hedges Masters quarter-final against Doug Mountjoy in 1985, Tony Meo was three times penalized for a miss by referee John Street, and was still short on his fourth attempt, which the referee allowed. In an exceptional case it might actually be impossible to hit the ball on. The striker must still do his best, even if he knows he is doomed to miss.

If in making a stroke, or preparing to make a stroke, a player inadvertently touches any ball with his cue or any part of his person or clothing, he has committed a foul, and the penalty is the value of the ball on, or the ball touched, whichever is the higher. These fouls are very difficult for the referee to spot, particularly when a striker just touches the cue ball when feathering. It is a convention, of which snooker players are justly proud, for a player committing such a foul to retire from the table and inform the referee of the offence.

If a player causes the cue ball to leave the table it is a foul and the penalty is the value of the ball on. His opponent begins his shot from hand, i.e. he may place the cue ball wherever he likes within the D. If any of the colours (yellow to black) leave the table, the penalty is the value of the ball on or the ball which leaves the table, whichever is the higher. The ball is re-spotted before the opponent begins his shot. If a red leaves the table, the penalty is the same, but the red is not re-spotted.

When a ball needs to be re-spotted and its own spot is occupied by another ball, it is spotted on the highest spot available, i.e. the black spot if possible, if not, the pink, and so on. If all spots are occupied, the ball is placed as near its own spot as possible in a line from its spot and the nearest point of the top cushion, without touching another ball. In the case of the black and pink needing to be re-spotted, it is possible, though rare, that such a spot will not be available, in which case the ball is spotted as near as possible to its spot in a line from its spot and the nearest point of the bottom cushion.

If a player pots the wrong ball, i.e. a ball which is not on, the penalty is the value of the ball on or the ball potted, whichever is higher. For example, if the player is on the pink and pots the black, the penalty is seven points; if he pots any other colour, the penalty is six points, the value of the pink. If the cue ball goes into the pocket in-off another colour, the penalty is the same. However, if the cue-ball hits the ball on first, and then goes in-off a higher colour, the penalty is the value of the ball on. For example, if a player is on a red, and the cue ball subsequently goes in-off the black after hitting a red, the penalty is only four points, not seven.

After potting a red, a player must play a colour, and is required to nominate it, although it is not usually considered necessary if it is obvious which colour is being played. However, the striker should certainly tell the referee the colour if there is any doubt. The referee will not ask. In a famous incident in the 1984 Coral United Kingdom semi-final, referee John Smyth did not hear Cliff Thorburn nominate a green, although some spectators did, and the television microphones picked it up. Cliff was penalized seven points, as if he had nominated the black.

If a player on a red pots two or more reds in the same stroke, he counts a point for each. This is not a foul, and the player continues his break in the normal way.

A foul which rarely happens at the top levels but is not uncommon among occasional players occurs when a player loses track of the situation and pots or attempts another red when in fact he has just potted one and is on a colour. The penalty is the maximum seven points. In other words, the referee assumes that the black is the nominated ball. On the other hand, if the player pots or attempts two colours consecutively, forgetting to pot a red in between, the penalty is the value of the ball played.

If the cue ball comes to rest touching another ball, the player must play the cue ball away from that ball without disturbing it. The break proceeds as normal. However, if a break ends with the cue ball touching a ball on, the referee will announce 'touching ball'. In this case the next player, while playing away from the ball on, will be deemed to have played it.

If a player is snookered after a foul stroke he is awarded a 'free ball'. In this case he may nominate any ball he likes as the ball on. If he pots it, it scores the value of the ball on. For instance, if a player is snookered on the reds by a foul stroke, he may nominate any colour to be regarded as a red, and if he pockets it will score one point and be on to a colour as usual. Any colour nominated in this way and potted is re-spotted. A player is regarded as snookered in this situation if he cannot hit both sides of the ball on. However, if the ball on is a red, a free ball is not given if the player cannot hit both sides of a red only because of the intervention of another red (often the case when the triangle is undisturbed).

An interesting point arising from this rule is that it is technically possible to make a break of more than the accepted 'maximum' of 147; in fact 155 is possible. If a player is snookered from a foul when all the reds are on the table, he can nominate a colour as his free ball, pot it (counting one), then pot the black, and then score 147 in the normal way. It requires, of course, something of a freak positioning of the balls before such a break is even possible, and even then its execution would be almost impossible. However, Kirk Stevens nearly achieved it in a televised match in 1984, missing the second last red with 152 'on'.

A player granted a free ball is not allowed to snooker his opponent in turn by means of the nominated ball. Such a stroke is a foul and the opponent will himself be granted a free ball.

After a foul shot, a player, whether granted a free ball or not, may ask his opponent to play again. This frequently happens at the top levels, where it carries a risk, of course, since a player asked to play again might, in fact, compile a break.

In all cases it is the player's responsibility to see that everything is in order (i.e. balls are re-spotted on their correct spots, and that he is not playing out of turn). It is not the referee's task to warn of an impending foul —

indeed he must not do so.

Cliff Thorburn was again a sufferer in a foul awarded when he played out of turn in a Hofmeister World Doubles semi-final in 1983. After opponent Tony Knowles had fouled, Cliff's partner John Virgo studied the table and asked Tony to play again, which he did. John sat down and Cliff got up and potted a red, only to be penalized. The order of play must remain unaltered throughout a frame, and John had not given up his turn by asking Tony to play again. Even if referee Peter Koniotes had been aware that Cliff was out of order before he played, he was not allowed by the rules to give him even a hint of what he was about to do.

A player may request the referee to pass him a rest, and to return it to its place after use, but it is the player's task to place the rest on the table and to remove it.

A colour-blind player is entitled to ask the referee the colour of a ball, and all players may ask the referee to clean any of the balls on the table.

When a game reaches the situation where only the black ball is left, the first score or forfeit ends the game, unless it brings the scores level, in which case the black is re-spotted and the players draw lots for the choice of playing the cue ball from hand. Many players are unaware of the rule when the following circumstances arise: a player, with only the black ball on the table leads by, say, five points. He then goes in-off or misses the black, giving him a deficit of only two points, with the black still on the table. He has, however, lost the game, on the 'first score or forfeit' rule.

These remarks cover only some of the more common 'knotty' points to arise in a game, and it is always a good idea when playing important matches to have a copy of the rules to hand. They are the copyright of, and available from, the Billiards and Snooker Control Council, Coronet House, Queen Street, Leeds LS1 2TN.

Peter Arnold

THORBURN'S CAREER HIGHLIGHTS

Cliff Thorburn was born in Victoria, British Columbia, Canada, and played first pool and then snooker. Years of pool-room hustling and money matches gave him the mental strength for which he is known as a snooker player. His preference for snooker was increased by seeing Fred Davis and Rex Williams in action in Toronto in 1970, the year in which the death of George Chenier left Cliff the leading player in Canada. The following year John Spencer, just about the best player in the world at the time, visited Canada and played Cliff in three long exhibition matches around the country. Spencer won all three (aggregate frame score 152-125) but the experience made Cliff determined to reach the top in world snooker. Spencer suggested he should come to England.

In 1973 Cliff turned professional and entered the World Championship, beating Dennis Taylor 9-8 in his first match, but losing to Rex Williams 16-15 in his second. These matches set a pattern for the future – nobody in world snooker gets involved in more matches which go to the last frame. Cliff is acknowledged as the hardest man of all to beat, which make his remarks on mental attitude in this book of particular value to aspiring champions.

In 1977 Cliff reached the World Championship final, losing to his old friend, Spencer, but in 1980 he became the first, and so far only, non-Briton to become World Champion in open competition. He tried living in England for a while to cut down his travelling for the big events, but the move was not a success and he reverted to 'commuting' from Canada. In 1987 he returned with his wife Barbara and sons Jamie and Andrew for another try.

In 1982 Cliff led Canada to victory in the World Team Classic, and in 1983 enjoyed the most famous moment in his career – the only 147 maximum break in the World Championship. His performance in this championship was extraordinary – he beat Terry Griffiths 13-12 in the second round after a final session of nearly $6\frac{1}{2}$ hours ended at 3.51 in the morning. He then beat Kirk Stevens 13-12 in the quarter-final and Tony Knowles 16-15 in the semi-final, in both matches taking the last three frames to win, before exhaustion caught up with him in the final.

Since 1980 Cliff has not been out of the top four players in the world. He is the only player to win the Benson and Hedges Masters, restricted to the world's top sixteen, three times. In 1984 he was awarded the CM (the order of Canada).

Not having had the benefit of textbooks when he was a young player, Cliff learned to play snooker the hard way, to some extent working out his own style. Having received so much from the game, he hopes that this book will return something to it and that it will help others to climb the ladder – perhaps to follow him all the way to the World Championship.

CAREER RESULTS

1971 North American Champion

1972 North American Champion

1974 Canadian Open Champion

1977 World Professional Championship
runner-up

1978 Canadian Open Champion
Benson and Hedges Masters runner-up

1979 Canadian Open Champion

1980 World Professional Champion
Canadian Open Champion
State Express World Cup (Canada runners-up)

1981 *Pot Black* Champion
Langs Supreme Scottish Masters runner-up
Tolly Cobbold Classic runner-up

1982 State Express World Team Classic
(Canada Champions)

1983 World Professional Championship
runner-up
Benson and Hedges Masters Champion
Jameson International runner-up
Winfield Australian Masters Champion

1984 Rothmans Grand Prix runner-up
Hofmeister World Doubles (runner-up with Willie Thorne)

1985 Mercantile Credit Classic runner-up
Benson and Hedges Masters Champion
Langs Supreme Scottish Masters Champion
Goya Matchroom Trophy Champion

1986 Mercantile Credit Classic runner-up
Benson and Hedges Masters Champion
Langs Supreme Scottish Masters Champion
Canadian Professional Champion (for the 13th time)
BCE International runner-up

1987 Tuborg World Cup (Canada runners-up)

INDEX

Made in United States
Troutdale, OR
10/09/2023

13543316R00080